Kilmany in Fife:

GLIMPSES OF HISTORY

David Weekes

Lavender Inprint
London

Published in 2013
by Lavender Inprint
235A Rotherhithe Street, London, SE16 5XW
to whom any communications should be addressed by e-mail:
lavender.inprint@gmail.com

Privately printed in 1988

This Edition first printed in 2013
with slight amendments.

The Reverend David Weekes
asserts the moral right to be the author
of this publication.

Copyright © David Weekes

ISBN 978 - 0 - 9565501 - 3 - 2

Other titles by the same author include:

The Origins of Lexham Gardens and Lee Abbey in London (1995)

A Short Description of Kilmany Parish Church (2009)

A Short Guide to Kilmany Churchyard, Fife (2009)

ΧΡΙΣΤΟC ΝΙΚΗΣΕΙ On John Buchan's Grave (2010)

How Captain James set Churchill on the Path to Glory (2010)

What Sir William Fettes Really Meant (2010)

DEDICATED

To My wonderful Family

JEAN RICHARD CATRIONA AND ROBIN

Explanatory Note: My Darling Jean, ever beautiful and resourceful, then the mother of two young children aged three and eighteen months, came with me to Kilmany in 1968. In the following year they all valiantly set out to spend four years in Uganda amid many 'alarms and excursions.' Kilmany provided the refuge when we came home on leave and on our return. Here we all brought Robin back triumphantly from Craigtoun, and in the years since then it has ever been the constant refuge to return to from wherever our later wanderings have taken us.

Laus Deo.

Cover photograph – showing the Church and cottages (now Tack room) by Easter Kilmany. Here Norman Bluff has cared for horses for over fifty years. Into the 1970s there was an old painting of the Church viewed like this in the Vestry. It has since disappeared.

ACKNOWLEDGMENTS

All the illustrations are by the author, or from items in his possession including old photographs. Some are of poor quality because they have only survived as photocopies. Moreover, others are copyright and reproduced by permission. The Librarians at the Local History Centre, Dundee Central Library kindly gave permission to reproduce copies of the eight plates 15, 20, 25, 26, 27, 28, 30 and 35, taken at Kilmany on 21 April 1894, from the Wilson Collection in their care. Alan Grieve generously made available those of his grandparents and of Mrs Brown. For a small fee The Transport Treasury gave permission to include those taken at Kilmany and St Fort stations. The Frazer painting is from a photograph on page five of *Scottish Art Thursday 19 April 2012 at 2pm Edinburgh,* a catalogue supplied by Bonhams in that city. The Melville Brass etching is courtesy of the Society of Antiquaries of Scotland. Many years ago the author was given a negative of the image of the Smithy in 1885 which has been published elsewhere. Over many years the Reference Librarians in Cupar, and the staff at the Archives (now Special Collections) in the University of St Andrews have been unfailingly helpful in facilitating the obtaining of items connected with this research. For generous help in the production of this book the author is very greatly indebted to Professor Saleem Bhatti of the University of St Andrews, and to Ernest P. Clark, Jr., of St Mary's College in the same. Any errors that remain are the responsibility of the author.

Introduction

THE PARISH OF KILMANY

Described by The Reverend John Cook, Minister (1793)

The parish of Kilmany has the same name with that by which the most considerable village it possesses is distinguished. From a small burying-ground which surrounds the church, the name has probably been derived.

This village, which the name, the number of people it contains, and the vicinity of the church, distinguish above every other in the parish, is about 5 miles distant from Cupar, the county town, and that of the presbytery. It is scattered along the shallow and narrow water of Motray, which unites, in the westerly extremity of the parish, two small streams, issuing from different sides of Norman's Law, and which, after a short and gentle course, falls into the river Eden, not far from the bay of St Andrews.[1]

* * * *

The parish of Kilmany has almost disappeared. In all but name, it is now only an area defined on maps, or a civil or ecclesiastical identity lumped together with others. The Church of Scotland minister now serves a grouping of the once independent parishes of Creich, Flisk, Kilmany, Logie, and Moonzie, linked with Monimail. One told me recently that the area covered a hundred square miles of rural landscape which is now left without even a pub or shop and few people. As you drive through it there is little more to see than the glory of the undulating countryside, a scattering of farms with the occasional tiny village or hamlet. There are a few new houses dotted about but no such development. Thus it has always been, but in recent decades there has been loss. For hundreds of years there was a much greater sense of self-sufficiency, community and identity within this single parish centred on the Church.

---

1 *Statistical Account for Scotland*, Edinburgh (1793) pp. 420–421.

Often we cannot glimpse anything precise about events here, but only surmise them from what was happening within the wider locality which will have created a ripple or a storm within the lives of the parishioners and all too rarely perhaps a real sense of exuberance.

Some will ask what is there here to make a book about? Nobody of earth-shattering importance emerged from this pastoral backwater. Most of its sons and daughters lived lives of rural obscurity. Occasionally someone went out and acted upon a wider stage and achieved a limited notoriety or fame. Two or three who spent some years within the parish are still remembered in occasional references both local and national. Few past inhabitants have left us anything beyond the bare record that can be found more recently in census returns and before that in the church registers. Earlier than 1700 even these fail us, and before 1400 there is rarely a name that can be recovered with any certainty. Most are "perished as though they had never been."

Even so, some of us may feel that the poet who once wrote of "lives obscurely great" gives sufficient justification for the celebration of those to be found within the glimpses of history recorded in the following pages. Particularly may this be so as no one has previously published anything but the barest account for more than a century since Leighton and Millar compiled their histories of Fife (see below, notes 20 and 85).

*   *   *   *

This is **a** book that I have written about Kilmany, but it is not **the** book. Apart from a few emendations this one had been completed by 1988. During the following twenty years I discovered a great deal more about the dozen estates or farms within the parish, their owners and occupiers. I had virtually completed for publication a much fuller, and better, book when our Kilmany home was destroyed by fire in 2011. This fuller MS, together with the research notes and books upon which it was based, were consumed along with everything else. I have made some attempt to revisit those sources, but to complete the task again will be the work of years and may not be practicable.

This earlier work is full of imperfections. Too inclined to follow my own interests, and new details I had been discovering, it is not a balanced account. However, as nothing as full as this has been published about Kilmany, to start to fill the gap, to celebrate our return after a two year involuntary exile in St Andrews. and knowing its inadequacies, I make public what I still have to hand.

December 2012

NOTE ON LOCAL NAMES USED IN THE TEXT[2]

The names of estates or farms in the parish are printed in bold to distinguish them from places elsewhere. Spelling has varied over the centuries so that names printed here are not consistent, but are always recognisably the same.
- **Rathillet**: now a small secondary settlement in the parish.
- **Motray:** the burn which runs through the parish and hamlet of Kilmany.

---

[2] Anyone interested in Kilmany place-names cannot do better than consult the mine of detail in Taylor, S. and Márkus, G. *The Place-names of Fife*, Vol. Four, Donington (2010).

ILLUSTRATIONS

	Map of Kilmany Parish	xi
1	View over Kilmany	xii
2	Mountquhanie Castle	11
3	Mountquhanie Castle Ruins	11
4	Rathillet Old House	14
5	The Melville Brass	16
6	Straggling Huts	21
7	Marriage Lintel	21
8	Lochmalony House (front)	26
9	Lochmalony House (side)	26
10	Kilmany Church 1841	28
11	Kilmany Church Panels	29
12	Kilmany Church Interior	30
13	Baptism Bowl and Hour Glass	30
14	Easter Kilmany Farmhouse	35
15	Kilmany Manse 1894	36
16	Mountquhanie House	40
17	Coach Road	45
18	Kilmany Cottage	49
19	Improvements in Housing	54
20	Kilmany Sawmill 1894	55
21	The United Presbyterian Church at Rathillet	57
22	David Brewster	59
23	Kilmany Flour Mill	61
24	Kilmany Smithy 1885	62
25	Kilmany Church 1894	65
26	Kilmany Smithy 1894	65
27	Kilmany School 1894	67
28	Kilmany School Children 1894	67
29	"Fife". Colonel Anstruther Thomson	68
30	Kilmany Cottage 1894	68
31	Kilmany House	69
32	Colonel Anstruth-Gray's New Road	70
33	Robert and Elizabeth Grieve	71
34	Kilmany Letter Box	71
35	Kilmany Smithy Complex 1894	73
36	Kilmany Station	74

37 The Locomotive	74
38 The Oil Lamp at St Fort	75
39 St Fort Station	75
40 Jim Clark	78
41 Kilmany Station (Disused)	81
42 The Reverend Jack and Mrs Nancy Scroggie	81
43 The Museum and Laundry	82
44 Cottages and Bothy	82
45 Mrs Brown and Mrs Grieve	84
46 Squash Court and Dairy	85
47 The Newburgh and North Fife Railway	87

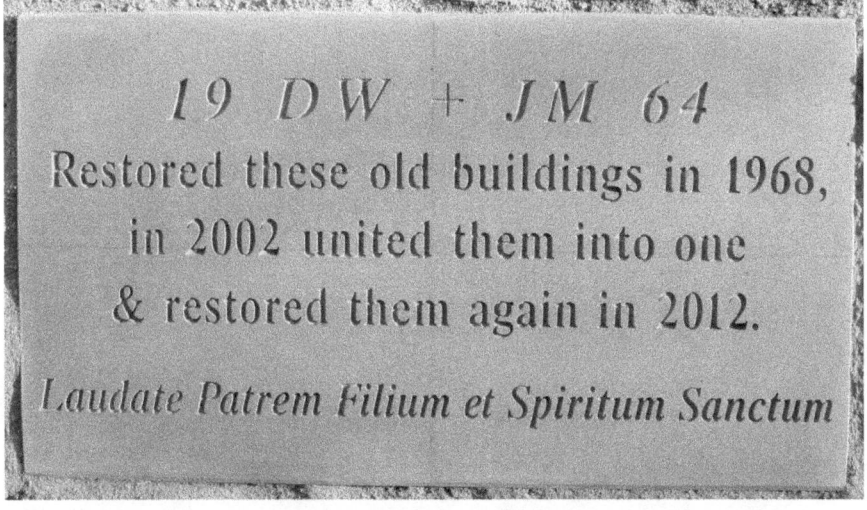

KILMANY. A recent commemorative stone: traditional marriage lintels might include more than initials and date. There are some fine examples of such in nearby Falkland.

SOME PRINCIPAL CHARACTERS MENTIONED

Literary Travellers in these parts

Daniel Defoe (*circa* 1660–1731)
Richard Pococke (1704–1765)
Samuel Johnson (1709–1784)
Sir Walter Scott (1771–1832)
Robert Louis Stevenson (1850–1894)

Some Ministers of the Parish

John Sharp (1601–1605)
James Thomsone (1611–1647)
John Cook (1793–1802)
Thomas Chalmers (1803–1815)
Henry David Cook (1815–1857)

Landed Proprietors (Heritors) of the Kilmany Estate

John Thomson of Newton, afterwards of Charleton (*circa* 1711–1785)
John Anstruther Thomson of Charleton and Kilmany (1776–1833)
grandson of the above
John Anstruther Thomson of Charleton and Kilmany (1818–1904)
elder son of the above
William Anstruther-Gray of Kilmany and Carntyne (1859–1938)
second surviving son of the above
Sir William John St Clair Anstruther-Gray,
afterwards Lord Kilmany (1905–1985)
only son of the above

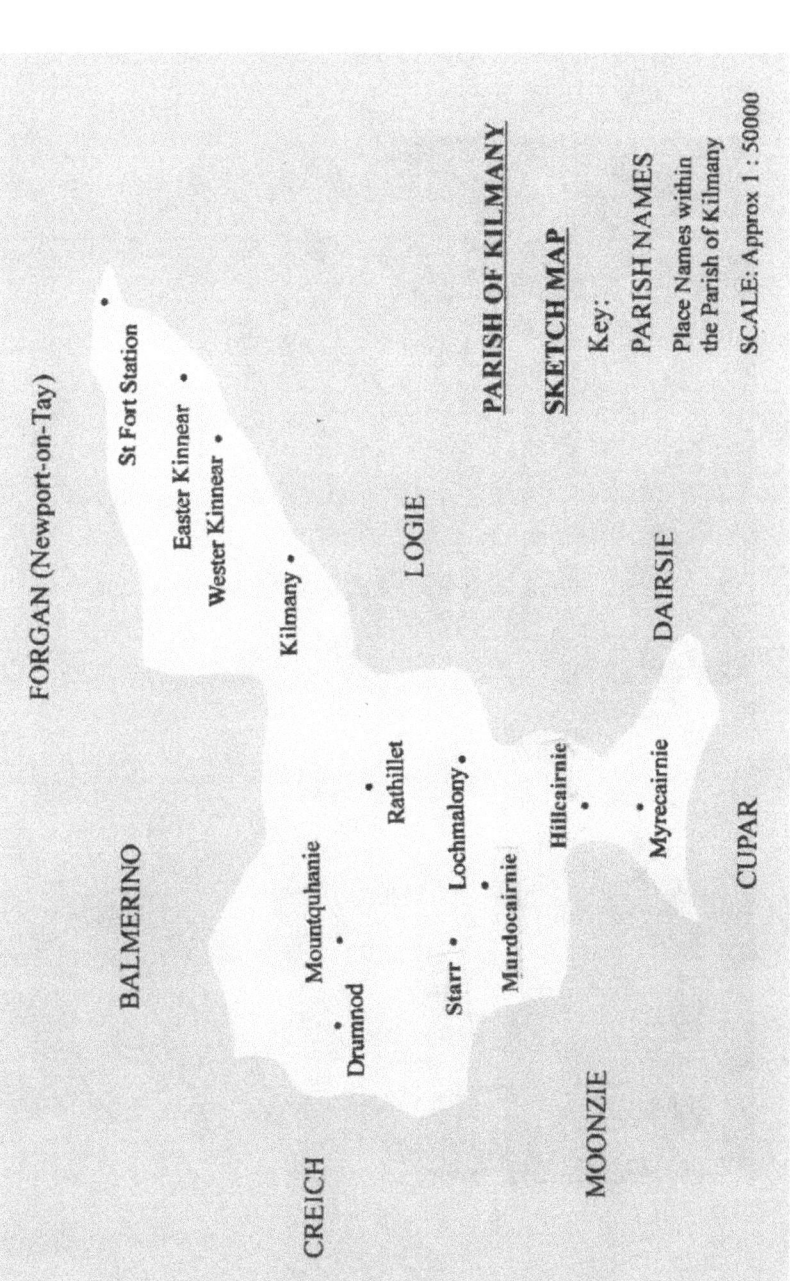

THE A92 runs right across from St Fort via Kinnears, Kilmany and Rathillet to Starr.

1 A VIEW OVER KILMANY towards Balmerino. The amphitheatre as described on page 1.

KILMANY IN FIFE: GLIMPSES OF HISTORY

On the 29th August 1760, Richard Pococke, Bishop of Ossory (and later of Meath), travelling through Scotland, came from Newburgh to Balmerino. Having explored the Abbey ruins, he then set out for Cupar by climbing the hill to the south, and "came into a beautiful Amphitheatre between the hills out of which rise several streams and fall into the Eden, and crossing over a hill came in four long miles to Couper."[3]

That "beautiful Amphitheatre" is the strath and parish of Kilmany (for the name belongs to the whole and not just to the small hamlet which also bears the name). But in the past we must imagine it having a rather different aspect: bare topped hills, undrained valley bottoms, crops confined more to the lower slopes; and earlier still "there were innumerable lochans and bogs and marshes"[4] and above them "dense forests extended where all is bare or cultivated now",[5] which in time produced the great bogs of which Bishop Leslie writes in the 16th Century: "quhilke thaireftir in processe of tyme turned into that thicknes that it grew into fast eard" - that is into peat.[6]

From this date we could begin the story of Kilmany's development into modern times; but first let us take a glimpse into even more distant days. For everything before the beginning of the Sixteenth Century we must depend mainly upon what can be known about life in North Fife in general rather than specific information relating to the exact boundaries of what eventually became delimited as Kilmany parish. The earliest people known in this area belong to the Mesolithic period roughly between 9,500 and 5,500 years ago. These were nomadic hunter gatherers from land and water using stone or bone weapons, and they functioned during a period of

---

3   Pococke, R. *Tours in Scotland 1747, 1750 and 1760*, Edinburgh (1887 edition), p. 265; Bishop of Ossory, 1755–65.
4   Wilkie, J. *The History of Fife*, Edinburgh (1924) p. 15.
5   *Ibid.*
6   Leslie, Bishop J. *The Histories of Scotland*, (translated by Father J. Dalrymple) Edinburgh (1888) Vol. 1, p. 36.

climatic change and oscillating sea levels. The land was forested with birch, hazel, elm and a little later with oak and pine too. Clear evidence of their activity has been found locally at Fife Ness and in particular at Morton, over towards Tentsmuir. This shows that people there gathered raw materials from a wide surrounding area. Though nothing can be said about their presence in what is now Kilmany, there can be really no doubt that they were active here too.

The Neolithic period began about 5,000 years ago and was characterised by the presence of farming, The *Cursus,* identified from aerial photographs, is from this time. Composed of ditches eight meters apart and a hundred meters in length, it runs ENE-WSW near the road (A92) opposite Wester **Kinnear** farmhouse. Its purpose is still uncertain.

From within the Prehistoric period also came the carvings on a "rounded boulder of trap" at **Lochmalony**. Its purpose is also unknown. This 'cup and ring stone', first described in 1872, had survived there for upwards of 3,000 years but was lost for ever when the farmer dynamited it in the 1960s.

The Bronze Age followed, and then the Iron Age. To the last period belong the prehistoric hill forts like that on Norman's Law, the highest point in North East Fife, which is just outside the parish, and probably also the small open settlement of three round stone-walled houses at nearby **Drumnod**, just within it.[7]

Early nineteenth century belief that Agricola's great victory over 30,000 Britons around *Anno Domini* 80 took place in Fife, and that the mysterious Mons Graupius is to be identified with West Lomond, have now been exploded, but certainly there has long been thought of a Roman victory in Fife, so that we would imagine survivors straggling through this valley to evade pursuit. However, more recent research suggests that local people had some kind of *rapport* with the Romans, who thus posed no violent threat, so that their activity in the locality here was peaceful. Forts like Norman's Law do not seem to have been used at that time, and there is no evidence of burning. The Romans were certainly on the coast and on the Tay estuary around Abernethy in the First century and had Third century

---

7   *Inventory of Fife* (1933) RCAHMS for the last two, and also Morris, R. W. B., p. 78 (illus. p. 80) for Lochmalony. The stone was 3 feet high and some 9×6 feet in dimensions. It bore "2 cups-and-one-complete ring (4 inches in diameter) and 27 cups."

camps at Auchtermuchty, now thought to have been reached from the Tay through the Ochills, and at Edenwood on the river a couple of miles south-west of Cupar. Rather than imagining Romans pursuing the vanquished, it seems that we would be better to think of their presence only to ensure that they levied the requisite contribution of grain from the farms of the indigenous people. Nevertheless the reality of having foreign soldiers in the land can hardly have been solely benign. The demands of feeding them must have put a considerable strain on the resources of the local population not only in terms of grain, but of livestock, fuel and other raw materials.

Later, after the Romans, the white long-horned cattle of the Pictish people who used Norman's Law as a focal point and their fortress, or for some other purpose, would have grazed as far as this. There is local evidence for the presence of these people from the excavations at Easter **Kinnear** in 1989 and just across the A92 at **Hawkhill** below the Hotel (since restored to be **Sandford House** again) in the following year.[8] Both sites revealed scooped underground stone-built storages, which had been afterwards filled in and sometimes built on later. Evidence indicated that they had gone out of use by the 6th century. A citadel on the summit of Norman's Law probably belonged to the same period. At Hawkhill there were also indications of a medieval long-house.

Then there are the early Christian times when St Cainnech (Kenneth), a Pict of Ireland came to the Picts of Fife about 564.A.D. and having settled at Kilrymont (St Andrews), his influence spread inland; so that perhaps from these days came the place-names of celtic origin like **Mountquhanie**, still the principal mansion-house of the parish, a name which certainly derives from the nearby areas of marsh or bog, and **Kilmany**.

This then is a suitable point to inquire into the origin of the name which later came to designate the parish. Over the centuries there have been different spellings, *Kilmanyn,* apparently in 1250, *Kilmainy* in 1518, and *Kilmeny,* as it is still pronounced, was certainly inscribed on eighteenth century Communion tokens. There is no doubt that the name has a Celtic source, and the compilers of

---

[8] Driscoll, S. T. 'A Pictish Settlement in North East Fife: the Scottish Field School of Archaeology Excavations at Easter Kinnear' *Tayside and Fife Archaeological Journal*, 3, (1997) p. 112.

works on Scottish place-names centre first on the widespread pre-fix *Kil-* and variously derive this from the Gaelic *cille*, for a cell or church, or *coille,* a wood. The second part of the word has been attributed to the name of an Irish leader who owned the wood, or to a Christian saint such as St Mannan or more often St Eithne, the mother of Columba. The last attribution seems inexplicable unless it is pointed out that it derives from *cille*, together with *m'*, an abbreviated form of *mo*, meaning my, followed by *Eithne*. However, there is no known reason why either should have been the dedicatee of the church in this place. Altogether such conjectures leave us with a number of possibilities: the cell of the monk, the church of St Mannan or of St Eithne, the wood of an Irish lord, or even simply hillock wood.

An authority on Scottish Place-names, W. F. H. Nicolaisen, wisely observes that "it is not always easy to sift the *cill*-names proper from those which in their anglicized form look identical but, when properly examined, are found to contain such elements as *coille* 'wood'." He notes that "one of the main criteria in this respect has, of course, been the presence of a saint's name as the second element....."[9] Another contemporary scholar, Simon Taylor, also has an interesting paragraph which involves Kilmany:

> There is no doubt that by the 8th century a mature and well-organised Pictish Church had developed, fusing together influences from Dál Riada (Argyll, especially Iona). Ireland to the west, and Northumbria to the south. The beginning of the 8th century was a complex time in Pictish Church history, and it is probably during this period that the eleven Fife place-names were coined which contain the Gaelic *cill* 'church'. They form a remarkable cluster centred on east Fife, the only area on the whole east coast of Scotland, south of Inverness to contain *cill*-names. ... Of these eleven names, seven would eventually designate Medieval parishes, which shows their ecclesiastical significance.[10]

Both the eleven, and the seven, include Kilmany and this seems to clinch the argument in favour of the *Kil-* derivation being from the

---

9   Nicolaisen, W. F. H. *Scottish Place-names: and their Study and Significance*, London (1976) p. 129.

10 Taylor, S. in Omand, D. *The Fife Book,* Edinburgh (2000) p. 212.

Gaelic for a church or cell, rather than for a wood. Both men agree that such names were established between the seventh and ninth centuries, and Nicolaisen argues strongly for a date between c.650-800 for their emergence.[11]

The source of -*many* is not clear. Though belief in the derivation from St Eithne still persists, the dedication to such a saint in North-Eastern Fife, or indeed to St Mannan who was known in Wexford, remains unconvincing. The best that we can say here about a name first given not less than some twelve hundred years ago is this: given that prior to the eighteenth century the present banks of the Motray water extended widely into a lake and marshland, the long-standing ecclesiastical site at Kilmany would, on dry and slightly higher ground, have provided a refuge for a monk (Gaelic *cille,* plus *manach,* 'monk', [Latin *Monarchus*]) or saint, whose identity is now unclear, and where a church had been established by the time of the Middle Ages.

These Pictish people lived in Eastern Scotland extending as far south as the Forth. They had a kingdom centred on Inverness and another in the south. By the 8th Century St Andrews (Kinrimond or Kilrymont) had emerged as the southern centre.

Long ages of sporadic raiding and trading by Danish as well as Norwegian Vikings, remembered in place names such Norman's (Northman's) Law, followed the coming of the Pictish Christians. Here on the east coast of Scotland they were marauders who tended to use navigable rivers such as the Tay to reach for plunder inland. Evidence of this threat is found in the hoards of concealed treasure which survived to be rediscovered in modern times. Found only a few miles away, one such is the Lindores hoard dated about 1025 and consisting of silver coins some of which are from the reign of King Cnut.[12] However, the very real threat of the Normans brought more settled days when, soon after the Conquest, the refugee Saxon princess Margaret was married in Dunfermline to Malcolm Canmore, King of Scots, last of the strong Celtic monarchs.

In these ancient times the whole of the land belonged to the Crown, the Church or to an individual who held it from the King.[13] In about 1160 Canmore's son, Malcolm IV (1153–65), bestowed

---

11 Nicolaisen, *op. cit.* p. 130.
12 Ritchie, A. *Viking Scotland*, London, (1993) p. 105.
13 Wilkie, J. *The Benedictine Monasteries of North Fife*, Edinburgh (1927) p. 6.

Rathillet as a royal dowry on Duncan, II, Thane or Earl of Fife when he married a lady who seems to have been of Norman descent. These indigenous Earls needed to become identified with the new, strongly influential Norman families, and secured this by marriage into the de Varenne family already so closely associated with the Scottish royal house.[14] The Anglo-Norman influence, which already dominated the neighbouring lands of Balmerino held by the Revells, Naughton by the de Lascelles and Leuchars, with de Quincys installed *circa* 1165,[15] was not now absent from Kilmany. The secular barony of Rathilletshire had its *caput* at Rathillet, where the site of the hall of the manor has been located. Duncan probably established the ecclesiastical parish co-terminus with this in which **Kilmany** Church already existed. The name is first recorded about 1202 when the Earl, who up to this time had been its patron, now resigned this right to the Bishop of St Andrews with certain rents in "the vill of Kilmany."[16]

Moreover, in this period great institutions and people began to appear in the vicinity of Kilmany. At the end of the Twelfth Century the first of the Benedictine Abbeys of northern Fife had been founded by the Tironensians at Lindores, a dozen miles to the west. Some thirty years later the second was begun at Balmerino, three miles to our north, by the Cistercians under the influence of Queen Ermengarde and her son Alexander II (1214–1249).

This same king had given the lands at the eastern end of the parish of Kilmany to a man who took his name from them. The area

---

14 Rathillet was granted to Duncan II, Earl of Fife along with Strathmiglo, Falkland, Strathbaan and the whole ferm of (King's) Kettle, charter dated between 20 November 1160-13 September 1162. It is printed by Sibbald (1710) and by Barrow, G. W. S. (Ed) in *Regesta Regum Scottorum* The Acts of Malcolm IV King of Scots p.153-165, Edinburgh (1960) No. 190, pp. 228–229. Barrow discusses the problems with this charter and its authenticity, *Proceedings of the Society of Antiquaries of Scotland*, lxxxvii (87) pp. 52–54. Earl Duncan II married a lady called Ela. Although for the present her parentage remains uncertain, it seems likely that she was a daughter of Reginald de Varenne, ancestor of the Warrens of Wormegay and brother of Ada de Varenne mother of Scottish Kings Malcolm and William.

15 Taylor, S & Henderson, J. M. 'The medieval marches of Wester Kinnear, Kilmany Parish' *Tayside and Fife Archaeological Journal*, **4**, (1998) p. 233.

16 Driscoll, S. T. 'A Pictish Settlement in North East Fife: the Scottish Field School of Archaeology Excavations at Easter Kinnear' *Tayside and Fife Archaeological Journal*, **3**, (1997) p. 112. Taylor and Márkus, *op. cit.* pp. 456 & 470, and p. 445 for the settlement of 1202.

is still known today as Easter and Wester (or Little) **Kinnear**, and Simon de Kyner founded a family which later became styled Kinneir of that Ilk. Shortly afterwards Simon gave Wester Kinnear to Balmerino Abbey. This was in about 1234, very soon after it had been founded. The charters conferring the lands record a "Sir Adam, chaplain of Kilmany" and other contemporary documents reveal a lord referred to as Hugh de Kilmany, a name which also seems to confirm the Norman presence among the feudal leadership,[17] (perhaps in a redistribution of land after the end of the first line of Earls of Fife). From the same century comes the fortified tower house or castle of Easter Kinnear, the scant remains of which are still marked on present day maps a little to the west of the farm house.

The creation of the nearby Abbeys brings to our attention the needs of pilgrims who made their way to notable shrines and holy places. One such was at St Andrews and pilgrims coming from the north who travelled by way of the Abbey farm at Grange of Lindores and Holy Trinity, Moonzie, in both of which places they could find hospitality, will then have come to Foodieash and on over Dairsie bridge to St Andrews by way of Strathkinness. These then will have passed just beyond the southern fringes of Kilmany parish, but those who came by way of Balmerino must have found their forward path passing through it.

Violence came again when Wallace defeated the English under Aymer de Valence at Black Earnside, not far from Lindores Abbey on 12 June 1298 (there is a commemorative sign in a lay-by on the Tay side road before Newburgh). However, thereafter the action moved away south and to Wallace's decisive defeat at Falkirk six weeks later.[18] Nevertheless the civilising forces of the church and the abbeys persisted. About 1410 teaching started in Scotland's first University at St Andrews and, forty years on, Bishop Kennedy placed the church of Kilmany under its patronage. He also endowed his College of St Salvator with the teinds (tithes) of the parish of Kilmany to form a common fund for the use and maintenance of all

---

17 Taylor and Henderson, *op. cit.* p. 242. At the end of the Eighteenth Century the Kilmany lands came into the hands of John Anstruther Thomson. Through the Anstruthers, this later laird was of Norman descent also.

18 Wilkie, *op. cit.* (1924) p. 207.

the foundationers.[19] One of the last Rectors of this church, James Bruce, was consecrated Bishop of Dunkeld in 1440 and four years later became Lord Chancellor of Scotland.[20] Within another thirty years St Andrews became the see of the Archbishop, Primate of Scotland and often a Cardinal.

In the next two centuries Kilmany stood close to key events in the land which too often would bring much bloodshed with them. In happier times, cries of the chase would be heard from Stuart kings out from Falkland who turned home from the hunt at Lucklaw hill, when there were still wolves and wild boar as well as deer roaming these acres.[21]

Terror came again when the English, victorious after Pinkie (1546), secure in the castle of Broughty Ferry, crossed over to Tayport and raided deep into Fife. They desecrated the Abbey of Balmerino which

> was ill to burn with its solid stonework, but the cottages and villages for miles around were more easily destroyed. No stack of corn, or hay, or straw that came within the purview of the raiders but went up in flames; no pile of wood or peat but was ignited. Miles away across the hills and waters men saw the glow in the winter sky that told how the English admiral kept Christmas.[22]

Norman, younger son of Balfour of **Mountquhanie**, helped in the murder of Cardinal Bethune (Beaton) that same year in the castle of St Andrews. It was of this Balfour family that Knox wrote: there was "neither fear of God nor love of virtue, farther than the present commodity persuaded them."[23]

Another fear, however, passed when the confrontation between reforming Lords of the Congregation and the Queen Regent's

---

19 Cant, R. G. *The College of St Salvator,* Edinburgh (1950), pp. 13, 37, 56, 63, 67, 71.

20 Leighton, J. *The History of the County of Fife from the earliest period to the present time,* Glasgow (1840) vol. II, p. 59. Bruces were Norman.

21 Wilkie, *ibid.* p. 265. The nearest we have been to the vestiges of that primeval world came when Richard and I walked up and on top of Ferret hill on a moon-lit midnight hour in August 1979 when the darkened stillness was eerily shattered by the bark of a fox, and there are still roedeer.

22 Wilkie, *op. cit.* (1927) pp. 305–306.

23 Leighton, J. *op. cit.* p. 59; see also pp. 38, and 94, 95, 96.

French a little beyond Cupar at Cuparmuir, ended in a truce signed on top of Wemysshall hill (modern Hill of Tarvit – NTS) in June 1559, and the threat to the locality melted away.[24] Nevertheless the Reformers reduced Balmerino Abbey to a ruin, and not much later John Knox and his cause triumphed at St Andrews. So we come to Bishop Leslie's time, in name at least the last Abbot of Lindores, and to the wars of religion and succession. Here came a dazzling moment in the story of our locality when in January 1564-65, the twenty-two year old Mary, Queen of Scots, widowed but not yet ruined, escaped from Edinburgh into Fife. By way of the great fortress of Ballinbreich, on the shores of Tay, she spent two days amid the destruction at Balmerino. Then on the 28th "mounted on her milk-white steed...she came riding up between the hills that guard the monastery and cantered across the moor to Kilmany" reaching St Andrews by evening to spend two of the last happy weeks of her life.[25] Within little more than two years she had left Scotland for ever. As her infant son and successor grew up as James VI there would be more tranquil times ahead.

The **Rathillet** lands had long before reverted to the crown, when the last earl of Fife was beheaded. They were then given to the Lindsays, earls of Crawford who bestowed them on cadet branches. Probably the most notorious of these was Alexander of Rathillet, younger brother of David, later eighth earl. In 1489 a number of these young Lindsays were out of all control. A feud broke out between two wild sons of the then earl who had been made Duke of Montrose. The heir, Lord Lindsay was wounded when he 'met in arms' his brother John, supported by the two cousins just named. Lord Lindsay died soon afterwards and six years later John succeeded his father in the earldom. This suspicious circumstance went unchallenged until 1512 when all three were charged with complicity in young Lindsay's death. Earl John was among the dead with his King at Flodden in the following year, and legal proceedings lapsed with the death of the principal. However, it is said that Alexander did not escape his fate because he died heirless, and his only illegitimate daughter was "a victim to seduction."[26]

---

24 *Ibid.*, p. 343.
25 Wilkie, (1927) *op. cit.* pp. 314–315.
26 Lindsay, A. W. C., *Lives of the Lindsays*, London (1849) Ch. VII, pp. 169–170 & 194 note.

Rathillet then passed to other Lindsays. One of this family, Sir David Lindsay, Lyon King of Arms from 1568 to 1591, and a relation of Sir David Lindsay of the Mount, was the proprietor in his day, and Provost of Cupar.

Thereafter Rathillet was soon acquired by another family with implications of murder on its hands. The Halkerstones were from a Lothians family. Sir Thomas had accompanied Alexander, illegitimate son of James IV and afterwards Archbishop of St Andrews on Continental tours in 1506-07. In 1544 his son and successor, Robert, was killed fighting the English in Edinburgh (celebrated still by Halkerston's Wynd) and Henry, his brother

> In contemplation of the almost continual devastation of his lands on the south side of the Forth from frequent invasions of the English, and to place his family in more safety from their future incursions and depredations, he began to sell their lands in the south, and to purchase lands in Fife, Hilcairnie, Grange, Rathillets Easter and Wester, Thorntoun, Wester Kinnear, & c. & c. This gentleman continued firmly attached to the interest of his misfortunate sovereign, Queen Mary in her distress.[27]

This family story may well be true but overstates the acquisition of all those lands in one generation. It is more likely that they were held in succession, for it was only in 1635 that his great grandson, James "of Hilcairney" (c.1615-1679) entered into possession of Rathillet which had recently belonged to Cunyngehames. He became Minister of Cleish in Kinross. We shall return to this family later.

The adjacent lands of **Murdocairnie** first came to the Melvilles of Raith from James V in 1536. Sometime after that King's death the laird was executed for treason, but his son had pleaded for the life of Mary, Queen of Scots and became a favourite of her son, James VI, who came to visit him at Murdocairnie during a progress of 1583. Made a judge, as Lord Murdocairny in 1594, some time after the union of the crowns he was raised to the peerage as Lord Melville of Monymail, which he had purchased, and on which a descendant would build the great house which still bears the name of

---

27 Halkerston, H. *Family of Halkerston of that Ilk*, Edinburgh (1777) p. 6.

the family.[28]

In medieval times the parish included several fortified houses. Apart from Easter **Kinnear, Murdocairnie. Myrecairnie** and **Rathillet** must have had them. Another was nearby at the now ruined castle of **Mountqhuanie**, a Balfour stronghold. Originally built in the fifteenth century, a surviving stone inscription of 1597 indicates that the structure was still being extended at that time. In the 1980s the remains of this ruin were described thus:

> The roofless C16 tower survives. Simple three-storey rectangle, it has corner turrets and corbelled parapet. Vaulted ground floor inside. ... An L-plan west extension was added in the C17. Its two storey jamb still stands as a separate house. Conical-roofed SW tower incorporating a doocot.[29]

On a more domestic note, the nearby lands of **Myrecairnie** were held by Andrew Wemyss, and had been in the Earl of Wemyss' family for two hundred years. He was one of the early Senators of the College of Justice with the title of Lord Myrecairnie, and in 1595 the other Lords excused him from judicial duties for twelve days because of the lateness of his harvest.[30]

2 MOUNTQUHANIE CASTLE
Seventeenth century additions with the old tower behind.

3 MOUNTQUHANIE CASTLE RUINS
Abandoned after Mountquhanie House was built. (See illus. 16, p. 40.)

A new century opened with John Sharp becoming Minister at Kilmany but he did not remain for long in his charge. Defying the

---

28 Melville House; *Oxford Dictionary of National Biography (ODNB),* **37** pp. 786–787. Melvilles were another Norman family.
29 Gifford, J. *Buildings of Scotland: Fife,* Edinburgh, (1988) p. 326.
30 Leighton, *op. cit.* Vol. II, p. 55.

express command of England's first Scottish King, James VI and I, Sharp was one of the nineteen ministers who attended the Assembly at Aberdeen in July 1605 and was appointed their clerk. With five others he was charged with treason, imprisoned for over a year, then banished for life.[31] His successor too, was strong for the reforming cause. James Thomsone became the great friend of Alexander Henderson "yellow from the fever of the Leuchars marshes"[32] and Minister there, who emerged as the real leader of the Covenant. Shortly before they both died, Henderson sent Thomsone from London a copy of his *Directory for Worship,* dated 20th March 1645 and inscribed with this dedication:[33] "To my reverend and deere brother Maister James Thomsone, minister at Kilmainy, in remembrance of my constant affection, till God bring us to his own immediate presence, when we shall not need any Directory." The tombstone to Thomsone (1566-1646) can still be seen and it is perhaps the oldest visible thing in Kilmany churchyard. Originally on the ground, it is now built into the extreme west end of the south side of the church, and commemorates him and his wife of forty-one years, Bessie Smith. Though very badly weathered, his name can still be made out. He was joined in the ministry at Kilmany by his second son, George, who continued in office here after his father's death.[34]

He had no sooner succeeded to the charge in 1646 before being involved in a difficult matter, some details of which survive. Two of his parishioners, Janet and Marie Mitchell, or Mitchells, had been accused of witchcraft by Grissel Thomsone, about whom little is known except that she had already been executed as a witch herself somewhere within the local presbytery of Cupar. It was a hard and risky matter to try to clear one's name in such circumstances, but harder still to go on living under accusation even when nothing else was officially known against them. Janet and Marie therefore asked that they be cleared of suspicion. This involved appearing publicly

---

31   Scott, H. *Fasti Ecclesiae Scoticanae,* Edinburgh (1925) Vol. V, p. 160.

32   Buchan, J. *Montrose,* London (1931 edition) p. 89.

33   Aiton, J. *The Life and Times of Alexander Henderson,* Edinburgh (1836) p. 105 note, and p. 106 note.

34   Cook, H. D. Article on Kilmany Parish (June 1838) in *New Statistical Account for Scotland,* vol. V, p. 542.

before the congregation where it was proclaimed that nothing but "that quilk that wretche spak" was known, and so a period of two weeks was set for anyone to speak up in support of the charge. In the absence of any such development they were restored to communion in the church. George Thomsone was a key figure in all this, not only as the parish Minister, but also in his enquiries within the wider church about how best to proceed.[35]

Perhaps Kilmany was not too scathed by these troubled times of the Covenant, the Civil War, and its aftermath. The routine of parish life went on. Though a very small part of this, and rather an aberration, there was another incident involving charges of witchcraft twenty years later. This time two people called Brounes were apparently self-confessed.

But there were horrors of a different kind, and one local name and one nearby house echo down the centuries and haunted the youth of Robert Louis Stevenson. In 1679 David Halkerston (or Hackston) left his house and lands of **Rathillet** and in the name of the Covenanting cause was present at the murder of the Primate of Scotland. Archbishop Sharp, bitterly hated throughout Fife, was travelling back to St Andrews when, almost in sight of home, he was attacked on Magus Muir near Strathkinness by nine armed men. They were led by Hackston and his brother-in-law, Balfour of Kinloch (near Collessie, about ten miles from Kilmany). The Archbishop was attended by his daughter and servants, but no armed men. The killing lasted for nearly an hour. Hackston took no part. He had a personal grievance against the primate and would not give grounds for any belief that he was settling this by the murder. Daniel Defoe, a Londoner who was alive at the time, recounted how "Hackston of Rathellet, who was not willing to have his Hand in the Blood, though he acknowledg'd he deserv'd to die ... went off and stood at a distance."[36] He further chronicled the curious irony that "none of the Murderers ever fell into the Hands of Justice, but this Hackston of Rathellet, who was most cruelly tortur'd, and afterwards had his Hands cut off, and was then executed at Edinburgh though he took no part." For Stevenson writing two

---

35 MacDonald, S. *The Witches of Fife*, East Linton (2001) pp. 48–49. Baxter, C. (Ed.) *Selections from the Minutes of the Synod of Fife*, Edinburgh (1847)

36 Defoe, D. *A Tour Thro' the whole Island of Great Britain*, London (1727) Vol. III p. 160.

4 RATHILLET OLD HOUSE. Still there, tucked away in the farm steading at Rathillet, stands Old Rathillet House (centre rear with large door) from which David Halkerstone or Haxton, rode out to the killing of Archbishop Sharp in 1679. The old doocot stands in the foreground. The new house was built nearby over a century later, after the last Halkerstone had departed.

hundred years after the event[37]

> the figure that always fixed my attention is that of Hackston of Rathillet, sitting in the saddle with his cloak about his mouth, and through all that long, bungling, vociferous hurly-burly, revolving privately a case of conscience. ... It is an old temptation with me, to pluck away that cloak and see the face – to open that bosom and to read the heart. ... But whenever I cast my eyes backward, it is to see him like a landmark on the plains of history, sitting with his cloak about his mouth, inscrutable.

Both these great writers knew Fife. In Wapping, Daniel Defoe encountered a sea-faring man from the Fife coast who had just returned from an extraordinary adventure in distant seas. His name was Alexander Selkirk, and from the tale of his four and a half years solitude on the desert isle of Juan Fernandez Defoe wove the story of Robinson Crusoe. Defoe later made *A Tour thro' the whole Island*

---

37 Stevenson, R. L. 'Random Memories' in *Across the Plains*, London (1918 edition) pp. 118–119.

of Great Britain. His journey included a visit to

> Balmerinoch, of which Mr Cambden takes Notice, but we saw nothing worth our trouble, the very Ruins being almost eaten up by Time: the Lord Balmerinoch, of the family of Elphinstone, takes his Title from the Place, the Land being also in his possession; the Monastery was founded by Queen Ermengred, wife of King William of Scotland.[38]

This account was published in 1727, towards the end of Defoe's life which spanned the reigns of all the monarchs from Charles II to George I. He had joined Monmouth's rebellion in 1685, and William III's army four years later, as had the local Fife magnate, George, 4th Lord Melville who was a key figure in the Glorious Revolution of 1689. This ended the rule of the Stuart dynasty and established William and Mary on the throne, thus ensuring the Protestant succession. Later he was created Earl of Melville, and built the formidable show house in Monimail a few miles to the south of Kilmany. The family had moved there a century before from **Murdocairnie**, in Kilmany parish which was then given to a younger branch. Therefore it is sometimes wrongly said that the Earl was buried in the Melville family plot in Kilmany churchyard. The enclosure is still there in the north east corner, but after the manner of old burial grounds it has been used by other families later. It still contains the grave of John Melville of Cairnie who died childless in 1724 aged 38. When the sandstone chest tomb which still stands was in a dilapidated state towards the end of the Nineteenth Century, the brass from the top of this grave was rescued and put up inside the church where it can still be seen. It contains a long poetic lament by his wife, Mary. After the Latin inscription, these tender lines begin,

> In what soft language shall my thoughts get free,
> My dearest Cairnie, when I talk of thee?

and ends with the pledge, "My spotless faith shall be forever thine."[39]

She kept her word to him, and never remarried.

---

38 Defoe, *op. cit.* pp. 161–162.

39 Walker, R. C. 'Notes on a Heraldic Monument at Kilmany, Fifeshire', *Proceedings of Scottish Archaeological* Society, 31 (1897), pp. 94–98.

5 THE MELVILLE BRASS

The poem is surrounded by "eight probative quarters or proofs of nobility by four descents. This is probably unique in Scotland."[40] Mary Melville was an impoverished granddaughter of the Earl of Lauderdale. As a proud Maitland she was showing that she had made a worthy marriage.

---

40 I am grateful to the Society of Antiquaries of Scotland for permission to reproduce page 94 from their *Proceedings*, vol. 31 (1896–1897).

Now to return to Stevenson's account, he rather despised Fife. "It has no beauty to recommend it, being a low, sea-salted, wind-vexed promontory; trees very rare, except (as common on the east coast) along the dens of rivers; the fields well cultivated, I understand, but not lovely to the eye." Many would quarrel with this judgment, at least in respect of the East Neuk villages from Crail to Elie by way of Anstruther, However, he did go on to acknowledge that "it is of the coast I speak: the interior may be the garden of Eden",[41] a supposition that we would endorse.

He is on surer ground when he reflects that "History broods over that part of the world like the easterly haar. Even on the map, its long row of Gaelic place-names bear testimony to an old and settled race."[42]

So this troubled seventeenth century closed, and something of its disruption is seen in Henry Cook's record of 1838. "Little is known of the ecclesiastical state of the parish before 1697, but it is evident from a minute of session, May 7th 1707 that the sacrament of the Lord's supper for a long time had not been regularly dispensed,"[43] and the parish register survives only from about the date he first gives after which, despite political uncertainties and Jacobite risings, Kilmany became more tranquil.

Defoe's journey was nonetheless made at a time of great changes for this part of the kingdom. Slowly the Act of Union of 1707, which was so unwelcome, led to a greater Scottish prosperity in which Fife shared. Though "all Fife was now astir" in the '15, urgent Jacobite activity was mostly confined to the coastal parts. Ardour cooled and in the '45 only ten Fife lairds followed the cause, including a later Younger of **Rathillet** who had changed sides contrary to his father's devotion. The son of a sheriff for the county, much could be written of this Helenus, the last of the Halkerstons of Rathillet. A truly tragic figure, he was regarded in his day as a great eccentric but in reality he descended into insanity having given up his estate in return for a very uncertain annuity. He married the daughter of a Jacobite in exile. She was Barbara Maitland, grand daughter of the third Earl of Lauderdale, sister to the Mary Melville

---

41 Defoe, *op. cit.* pp. 161–162.
42 *Ibid.*
43 Cook, H. D. *op.cit.* p. 542.

of whom we have read, widow first of Sir Edward Gibson, and then of Captain Robert Baillie of Balmeadowside, Parbroath and Luthrie, both Fife lairds. Baillie had the tragic distinction of being one of the few British soldiers killed at the Battle of Fontenoy in 1743. Even after her marriage to Helenus, she still called herself Lady Gibson. Their only child, a daughter, was eccentrically baptised Charles,[44] the name of their fallen hero. After Culloden the neighbouring lands of Balmerino were forfeited and sold by the Government, and Arthur, sixth and last Lord Balmerino (and fourth Lord Couper) went to the block. Though for good reason, the last Lord's home was at Mountainhall in East Lothian and not on the lands of his name,[45] this local connection will have had a sobering effect hereabouts. Young Helenus had to "lurk" in the country for a time.

Kilmany did not entirely escape the activities of the rebels who followed Bonnie Prince Charlie. In October 1747, the Kirk Session met and

> The minister represented that the rebels having been in his house several times during the late rebellion, and [had] carried off some of his effects, he had put in places he had thought they would not suspect, some papers of value in his custody, particularly a bill of seventeen pounds sterling, belonging to the kirk session.[46]

Happily the bill was renewed and there was no lasting loss, but it was a very anxious time for an honest man, William Smibert, minister here from 1722 until his death in 1759, and perhaps the only incumbent of Kilmany who was also a local laird, for "he acquired the estate of **Lochmalony**."[47]

---

44 Local records.

45 *ODNB* **18** pp. 309-310. Inheriting Balmerino from his half-brother on 5th January, at Culloden in April; executed on 18th August 1746; making a spirited defence of the cause; refuting the charge that Prince Charles had ordered no quarter to be given; "having taken the sacrament this day I forgive...all my enemies" and "die in the faith of the Church of England which I look upon as the same as the Episcopal Church of Scotland in which I was brought up." Six bore that title, three were sentenced to death in their generation, but only the last was executed, having no heirs. These Elphinstones were said to be cursed for taking Church lands at the Reformation.

46 Cook, H. D. *op. cit.* p. 544.

47 *Fasti.*

When Bishop Pococke came into his "beautiful Amphitheatre" in 1760 a new age was opening, one aptly described by John Buchan: "with the end of the eighteenth century came the dawning of a new world. Scotland had set her house in order, her industries were entering upon an era of wide expansion, and her agriculture was rapidly becoming a model to all Britain."[48] With this agricultural change we will be much concerned.

Had you come from Edinburgh at this time you would have taken the ferry boat from Leith on the nine mile crossing to the jetty at Pettycur on the point just south of Kinghorn and then come on by coach. In 1773, an Englishman on "A Journey to the Western Highlands of Scotland" took this route, and so Samuel Johnson passed near the home of John Thomson, Esquire of Charleton. Thomson was an improving landlord who had built himself a new country mansion on the estate of Newton in Colinsburgh about 1760 and renamed it.[49] It is in the parish of Kilconquhar near the coast at Elie,[50] and Thomson "was also laird of the lands of Kilmany and Touch." Well into the second half of the Twentieth Century villagers in Kilmany still had to have dealings with the Factor at the Estate Office at Charleton to pay their feu. Of Thomson's three children, two died without heirs while the third, Grizel Mary, was married in 1774 without her father's consent. Her husband was Colonel John Anstruther, of the neighbouring family of Balcaskie, and Thomson took care that he should have no benefit from his property, leaving the estate to the couple's young son, John born in 1776. Indeed, though the colonel lived until 1815, John succeeded on his mother's death in 1797 and became John Anstruther Thomson, Esq. of Charleton and Kilmany, etc. Though the new laird seems to have been the key figure in agricultural developments around Kilmany village, such work was already achieved or undertaken in other parts of the parish. Writing in the first *Statistical Account* (published in 1797) the minister (1793-1802) John Cook, who was afterwards Professor at St Andrews,[51] concluded that "the Parish is the

---

48 Buchan, J. *The Kirk in Scotland*, Edinburgh (1938 edition) p. 63.
49 *Ibid*.
50 Thomson, J. Anstruther, *Eighty Year's Reminiscences*, London, (1904) vol. 1, p. 2.
51 *Fasti*.

residence of husbandmen. Agriculture is the universal employment; it is the source and substance of its few commercial transactions"[52] though he regrets the tendency of modern policy to effect the "annihilation of the little tenants scattered over the country" as proprietors find it convenient "to have a large and easily collected rent."[53]

It was said of John Cook that "his powers of extempore verbal criticism were unparalleled"[54] and with apt turn of phrase he can be spirited in his comment. His description of the village bears quotation:

> A little attention to the pleasing irregularities in the ground on which Kilmany is situated, and through which the rivulet flows, might have made it a beautiful picture of rural scenery. But how seldom has such attention either chosen the situations, or arranged the forms, of the largest towns! Accident or the idea of conveniency, which can seldom be hurt by a regard to beauty, is allowed to have in these matters too powerful an influence; and in the position of the straggling huts of this village, as in that of many other places, we have to lament the carelessness which can build in beautiful places of residence, and yet neglect to take advantage of the aids which the scenery at once furnishes and suggests, to decorate the dwellings of men, and from these thus decorated, to derive ornaments in addition to its own.[55]

Nevertheless improvements had already been substantial, so that "the amazing rise in rents may be some rule of judging."[56] The dwellings now incorporated into our home at Loaning Hill (next to Kilmany Church) would have been three or four little homes by this time, and the marriage lintel of 1762 may give an accurate date, or may have been included from elsewhere at a later time of re-building. Thus the "straggling huts" gave place to these "cottages, low-roofed with thatch or tile, where the shuttles speed to and fro, and you hear the melodious notes of an old psalm tune floating in

---

52 Cook, J. *ibid.*, p. 429: Article on Kilmany.
53 *Ibid.*, p. 430.
54 Leighton, *op. cit.* p. 62.
55 Cook, J. *op. cit.* p. 421.
56 *Ibid.*, p. 427 note.

6 STRAGGLING HUTS adapted from Slezer, J., *Theatrum Scotiae* (London) 1693, 'Cottages by Falkland'. This impression shows buildings in the distance which not unrealistically replicate the inn and the farm at Easter Kilmany as seen behind the straggling huts by the Church in Kilmany, described by Dr Cook in 1793.

7 MARRIAGE LINTEL of 1762 mentioned in Gifford, *op. cit.*, p. 262. In 1968 Hew Lorimer, RSA advised painting the weathered sandstone to preserve it. The door has since been made into a window.

the evening air when the web is left for the night."[57] Cook also expressed other concerns - the need for drainage and for woodland. We have already noted the "innumerable lochans, bogs and marshes" and Blaeu's map of 1667 shows the large area of "**Starr** Marshes" directly west of Rathillet.[58] John Cook's much younger brother, Henry David, was minister of the parish (1815-1857). Writing in 1838 he tells us that "Great improvements have been made within the last forty years in ploughing and draining; and they are still proceeding. Furrow draining which promises such happy results has been introduced. ..."[59] But draining meant both gain and loss and the gain was largely to the rich.

> The Motray was once famous as a fishing stream. Its course was not direct, nor its waters equally shallow, as they now are; but at every turn, there were excellent pools or crannies, where the finny race could harbour, feed, and grow to maturity. By the improvements in agriculture, its character, in this respect, is in great degree lost. It now assumes the aspect of a large even drain. As such, it has answered the excellent purposes for which it was cast. It has converted a large tract of marshy ground into rich and productive fields; but it has removed those corners and holes, where trout, pike, and minnows delight to dwell. The angler is now seldom seen on its banks; and when he does appear, his labour and patience receive a very poor return.

Clearly hereabouts draining had improved the land yield, but in the west of the parish problems remained.

> Rathillet mill presents an obstacle for improving one part of the parish. Its dam-dike prevents a proper level from being carried through the low lands of West **Rathillet**, and **Mountquhanie**, and **Stair** {sic}. The fields lying along this part of the Motray, which from their situation, should be the most productive in the parish, are almost always damp, and do not bear the crops of which they are capable. They are also exposed to be occasionally flooded. Were this obstacle removed and the lands properly drained, the

---

57 Wilkie, *op. cit.* (1924) p. 578. Though not referring to Kilmany, the quote is apt.
58 Blaeu, *Atlas: Fife Pars Orientalist,* 1667.
59 Cook, H. D. *op. cit.* p. 548, and p. 537 for the following long quotation.

difference betwixt the crops, which are now, and which would be raised upon these fields, would amply remunerate the heritors interested, in a very few years. All such obstacles are removed in the eastern part of the parish, and the consequence is, that the banks of the Motray, which was once marshy and of little value, are now dry, and produce excellent crops of grain and the best of pasture. What are called the Greens and the Haughs of Kilmany, were also occasionally overflowed with water. This was corrected some years ago, by giving the Motray a new and wider course, betwixt the mill and the church of Kilmany.[60]

Then in a more general way he enlarges upon the former state of the valley bottom.

> The valley itself presents some striking features. The lower part of it has been under water to a considerable length and depth. This is evident from the height of the sandy hillocks scattered through the lands of East Kinnear, and from the nature of the formation of the mound, upon which the village and church of Kilmany are built. From the elevation of these, above the bottom of the valley, the water must have stood 20 feet above the channel of the Motray. From the nature of the sand deposited, it is probable that the east part of the valley formed an extensive lake. The grains of it are soft and small, and do not resemble the hard sharp sand which is found upon the sea shore. The upper part of the valley has also been under water, but rather as a marsh than deep standing water. The shape of the different hillocks and mounds shows that the lake has been gradually formed; the sides of them rise with a gentle slope, and generally speaking, the tops of them are smooth.
>
> There must have been some barrier to the east of Kinnear, which prevented the Motray having free access to the ocean; but the precise place where it was cannot be ascertained. How it was removed, is equally uncertain; the height of the water, accumulated for ages, probably forced a passage for itself to the sea, and left the valley a morass, which it continued to be for ages. It is not above fifty years since a great part of it was drained, and converted into excellent arable land. There is a vague tradition that

---

60 *Ibid*, p. 549.

> there was once a passage boat upon this lake to Cruivie and Straiton, and in confirmation of this, it is stated that a small anchor was found when the meadows were first ploughed.[61]

Evidently, therefore, this draining took place towards the end of the eighteenth century, at a time when there was much similar activity in surrounding areas, the most extensive of which had involved the lands of Rossie, before Auchtermutchy, in which Dutch engineers were engaged. Much additional rich agricultural land was thus added.[62]

"Trees very rare" notes Stevenson in his dismissive comments on the coast of Fife,[63] and earlier writers took up a similar lament. Dr Johnson spent time to make strong comments on the lack of trees:

> From the bank of the Tweed to St Andrews I have never seen a single tree, which I did not believe to have grown up within the present century.... The oak and the thorn is equally a stranger, and the whole country is extended in uniform nakedness, except that in the road between *Kirkaldy* and *Cowpar*, I passed for a few yards between two hedges. A tree might be a show in Scotland as a horse in Venice.[64]

John Cook applied the same strictures to his parish of Kilmany:

> *Wood and Scenery* – This range of hilly ground, which diversifies in the most striking manner the southern shore of the Tay, which in some places swells in full unbroken masses, with variegated colouring, in others, raises suddenly upwards ragged fragments of uncovered rock, might, were the hand of improvements to perform its office, make this part of Fife a scene of the most luxuriant beauty. There are brows on these hills which the plough cannot reach, or where its labour would not be rewarded; which equally by their situation and their soil are fitted to rear timber.

This could so readily be improved, for

> How much would it add to the scene, were the rich corn

---

61 Cook, H. D.. *op. cit.* p. 533.
62 Silver, O. B. *The Roads of Fife*, Edinburgh (1987) p. 172.
63 Stevenson, R. L. 'Random Memories' *op. cit.* p. 114.
64 Johnson, S. *A Journey to the Western Islands of Scotland*, London (1775) pp. 15–17 (this quotation from a later edition).

fields to rise into the bottom of woods stretching with various length down towards the plain; were some of the barest summits to escape above their verdure; and were the beautiful waters of the Tay seen through openings thus made picturesque?

But he also noted that something was being done in the 1790s:
> covered with firs; 21 acres on the estate of **Lochmalony**, bear them in great perfection, and we may see them sealing some of the steepest hills in the neighbourhood.

Even so, he hoped for much more.
> It is but just to observe, that the spirit of raising wood seems now to awaken: several plantations have been of late made, and are still making in the parish, and its neighbourhood; and if the exertions are vigorously continued, in 20 years the face of this part of the country will be completely changed.[65]

Elsewhere the elder Cook noted that out of the 3,963 Scotch acres of the Parish only 747 were not "arable, the most of which commonly produce good crops."[66] Of the rest "only about 74 acres bear trees grown to a visible size"[67] and he remarks to the proprietors that "for planting, the larch is in a special manner recommended to their attention."[68] In driving about the parish today it can be observed that this instruction did not go unheeded, although the younger Cook bears out that even in his day, over forty years later, not enough afforestation was taking place.

> *Woods* – Along with the writer of the last Statistical Account, we have to lament the want of woods and plantations. With these judiciously scattered through the parish, and on the hill-tops, Kilmany would present a scene which the man of taste would delight to contemplate. But, by most of the heritors, little has been done to make it one of the most beautiful parishes in Scotland. From this censure, David Gillespie, Esq., and John A. Thomson, Esq. and Captain Pearson, are excepted. **Mountquhanie**, under the fostering hands of Mr Gillespie, has become a splendid residence. The woods planted by him, on the neighbouring

---

65 Cook, J. *op. cit.* pp. 422–424.
66 *Ibid.*, p. 425.
67 *Ibid.*, p. 427.
68 *Ibid.*, p. 428 note 90.

8 At Lochmalony House this five bay frontage was added by Major and Mrs Scott in the 1790s. As agricultural improvements brought greater prosperity, lairds either built new on nearby sites as at Mountquhanie and Rathillet or extended older houses as here or much later at Kilmany.

9 The view from the side shows the frontage to be only one room deep with further additions to the rear. The old laird's house is left rather curiously sandwiched between.

hills, to the north-west and south, are yearly adding to the charms of his estate. The state of **Kilmany**, in this respect, was equally improved by the correct taste of the late Mr Thomson. The hills which separate Kilmany from the Tay were planted by him, and are now clothed with trees. Walks were cut through them, from which the Tay, the Carse of Gowrie, and the Angus hills are seen.[69]

He also observed that "some fine trees are about the village and church of Kilmany" and of "the larch, the Scotch fir, the plane, the beech and the ash"[70] which he especially notes all but the larch are still in that vicinity.

When it came to enlarged claims for the remains of antiquity, John Cook could be rather scathing.

> A few pretty large stones, sunk in the top of one of its hills, have excited curiosity; and the genius of antiquarianism, unaided by the information which the country can afford, would probably find in them the remnant of camp or castle. The less splendid, but the more just account of the inhabitants, makes them part of some common decayed fence.

Something can here be said of this church. He rightly noted of "*Antiquities*-No ruins of any abbey or chapel, not even the fragments of any remarkable building, give solemnity to the scenery of the parish."[71]

This of course could be simply because the present Church is indeed on the ancient site as the name implies, and that rebuilding has occupied an identical location ever since. Certainly the church was here in the middle ages. Long neglect over a troubled two centuries brought a sudden collapse in the autumn of 1767, causing the heritors to provide a new building within a year.

Let us read John Cook (1793) again: "The church stands on a beautiful bank, rising gradually from the stream, which flows past it on the s.; is skirted on the w. by some tall ashes."[72] Now threatened, we still have one in that row of trees. Then the future Professor has some lively comment:

---

69 Cook, H. D. *op. cit.* p. 538. Pearson then owned Myrecairnie.
70 *Ibid*, pp. 538–539.
71 Cook, J. *op. cit.* p. 424 (both quotes).
72 *Ibid.*, p. 421

10 KILMANY CHURCH by Arthur Perigal ARSA (1841)

> As late as the year 1768 the church was renewed. The building is simple and neat: but unfortunately the long narrow form in which almost all the old churches in this part of the country are constructed, has been too much retained. It seems strange, that there should have been so prevalent a partiality to a form of building, of all others least suited to public speaking.[73]

But it has its charm, and its antiquity. If only to view it, go inside if you can.

Cook was a gifted man, but his immediate successor was more than remarkable, and for many Scots he has been regarded as a spiritual genius. Thomas Chalmers came to the parish from the village of Anstruther and the University of St Andrews with the sole ambition of biding his time to succeed to the Chair of Mathematics

---

73 *Ibid.*, p. 421 note. His brother describers it 40 years later (Cook, H. D. *op. cit.* p. 553). He fails to note that this shape was due to their medieval origins.

11 KILMANY CHURCH PANELS. These distinctive 'raised and fielded' oak panels remain in the south eastern corner of the Church. The present pine panelling was put in after the reconstruction of 1768, and possibly only when the present box pews were made in about 1860. These survivors may even belong to a time before the present building, since reconstruction was on the identical site.

in his College. God had other plans and in a few years through a deep conversion experience the changed Chalmers awoke the Sunday sleepiness that one would have supposed in such a rural scene. The lane outside was thick with people streaming up towards the church. They came from near and far, many even crossing the Tay in small boats from Dundee, all to hear Chalmers. It can be no surprise that within a few years he was called away to Glasgow and then to St Andrews, then to Edinburgh, and to change the life of Scotland.[74]

Chalmers was active in all kinds of ways in his later years at Kilmany. After his conversion he not only became a noted preacher, much in demand here and elsewhere, but he took an active part in promoting foreign missions, especially through the work of the British and Foreign Bible Society. He established a local branch

---

74 Chalmers' life is too well known to need a reference, but Blaikie, W. G. *Thomas Chalmers*, Edinburgh (1897) pp. 5–6 has the earlier bibliography.

12 KILMANY CHURCH INTERIOR looking west. These box pews and the two windows opposite the pulpit date from after Chalmers' time.

13 BAPTISM BOWL (1787) and HOUR GLASS hung on the Pulpit.

known as the Kilmany Bible Society despite the opposition of the heritors, and sought to encourage such work throughout Fife. Prior to 1811 he had often neglected parish affairs, being absent furthering his academic ambitions and his writing, as well as through long periods of illness. Now he focused on traditional additional areas of parish ministry: education, visitation, and poor relief.[75]

The change in the tone and in the effect of Chalmers' ministry can best be described in his own words:

> I am not sensible that all the vehemence with which I urged the virtues and the properties of social life had the weight of a feather on the moral habits of my parishioners. And it was not till I got impressed by the utter alienation of the heart in all its desires and affections from God; it was not until reconciliation to Him became the distinct and the prominent object of my ministerial exertions; it was not till I took the scriptural way of laying the method of reconciliation before them, that I ever heard of any of these subordinate reformations which I aforetime made the earnest and the zealous, but I am afraid at the same time the ultimate, object of my earlier ministrations.[76]

Almost all children attended the Kilmany parish school at **Rathillet** for six years. This involved instruction in reading, writing, Bible Study, arithmetic, and geography. Chalmers became a fervent believer in the benefits to the community of the shared values and mutual support which this gave. He visited the school regularly, assisting the schoolmaster, John Lees, and experimented with other educational projects as well. In 1813 he established a Saturday Bible School for the children inspired by the Sunday School movement in England. This began on a monthly basis, but almost at once was held every fortnight. Within a year he had published a help to such instruction which soon became widely used in Scotland. In 1812 he also began popular lectures on the Bible for adults on Sunday afternoons. The following year this increased to two lectures, one in the afternoon and another in the evening. These complemented his Sunday sermons, and all were now well attended.

The parish extends six miles from north-east to south-west, with

---

75 Brown, S. J. *Thomas Chalmers and the Godly Commonwealth in Scotland*, Oxford (1982) discusses such matters.

76 Hanna, W., *Memoirs of the life and writings of Thomas Chalmers*, Edinburgh (1849), Vol.1, pp. 431–432.

the breadth varying from 1 to 3 miles. Including the hamlets at Kilmany and Rathillet there were twenty-two settlements (or ferm-touns) within the parish. Chalmers visited each several times a year where he met with the tenants and labourers. As the heritors rarely attended such gatherings, he visited their households separately. The systematic visits to these homesteads enabled him to encourage regular family prayer and worship; he was made aware and able to deal with moral problems in the home such as violence and drunkenness; he was kept in touch with the welfare needs of the population and able to help obtain medical help, food and clothing where these were needed.

Parish poor relief often depended on local factors, but essentially relied on gifts to the parish which legally had to be assigned according to the joint decision of the kirk-session and the heritors. Chalmers desired to get rid of the legal aspects of relief so that it would be replaced by "a communal spirit of benevolence". He embarked upon his own scheme whereby legal lists and definitions for eligibility would be superseded by the application of anonymous private generosity. After the poor harvest of 1812, he was aided in this when John Anstruther Thomson of Charleton, the Kilmany heritor, secretly gave him £15 for the poor. Unlike statutory poor relief, the only requirements were genuine need and good moral character as judged by Chalmers. Nearly two years later he was able to discuss the results of this experiment, showing that several people had been enabled to keep their self-respect and regain independence without the public humiliation of applying for poor relief. Chalmers wanted to extend this discrete aid by being permitted to use parish poor funds in the same way, but this was judged illegal by the administrators.

Concern for foreign missions and the needs of the poor came together in a petition which is found among Chalmers' papers. It is headed a "Humble Petition of the Undersigned inhabitants of the Parish of Kilmany in the County of Fife" and states

> that your petitioners regret that in the recent treaty of Peace with France no provision has been made for the immediate abolition of the African Slave Trade and whilst they rejoice in the blessings of Peace, they look with disappointment and sorrow on the acquiescence of the British Government in the revival of a traffic which must carry all the atrocities of war into the habitations of an

unoffending people.[77]

In fairness something more should be said about the spiritual effect of Chalmers ministry. He was, after all, a Christian minister and his first duty was to preach the Gospel. Certainly after his spiritual awakening, or conversion, around 1810, the lives of people were transformed through the effects of his ministry. In the middle of the Nineteenth Century a slim volume was published by the Rector of a country parish in far away Essex. Curiously the title was *The Missionary of Kilmany*, but it was not about Chalmers himself. Rather it was "a memoir of Alexander Paterson with notices of Robert Edie", who had grown up together as boys in the village.

Paterson was born here in 1790, and received a rudimentary education at the school before getting employment as a herd under the tenant farmer of Easter Kilmany, David Edie. Chalmers had noted several reasons why the Kilmany poor were helped spontaneously outside of official poor relief. One of these was that tenants and labourers recognised a communal duty to help them. There is a charming description of the leisure activity of young Paterson:

> Naturally of a bland and kindly temperament, he occupied his leisure hours in the fields, knitting stockings for his favourites in the village; and, when the herding was over for the day, he might be seen in some neighbour's garden, especially in the little plots of some aged females, digging or raking or planting as earnestly as if he had been labouring for hire. The genial nature which thus early manifested itself, was to open for him in after-years many a door to the hearts of the abandoned and the forlorn.[78]

He was also influenced by an old man of humble background in the village known as "The Shepherd":

In the winter evenings he used to gather round him a little circle of eager listeners. It was noticed that in that circle the place of the young herd was rarely vacant. "What," was his mother's frequent and rather impatient inquiry, "what makes you go so much to the shepherd?" "The shepherd," he would reply, "has a better head than any of you: it would be telling you all if you were like him, he can repeat the Catechism from

---

77 Chalmers Papers CHA 6.22.2, New College, Edinburgh.
78 Baillie, J. *The Missionary of Kilmany*, Edinburgh (1853), p. 2.

beginning to end without missing a word!"

As he grew older he joined his father in the cottage industry of weaving, but by 1811, when he was twenty-one, this confinement in the home and working at the loom had made him ill with what was described as incipient consumption.

Now us let turn to the lesser subject of *The Missionary of Kilmany*. Robert Edie was the eldest son of Paterson's first employer, the Easter Kilmany farmer, and three years his junior. Nevertheless, as boys they became firm friends. Robert was away at school in Cupar, but as he returned each Saturday, Alexander would go out on the Cupar road to meet him "entering on the happy weekly Holiday."

At this point it is interesting to explore the difference between Paterson's poor labouring background and the expectations of those who grew up in the family of a tenant farmer. This is already reflected in Alexander's rather meagre education compared with the much fuller one which Robert will have received in Cupar. The Kilmany churchyard still possesses the family stone.[79] This recorded David Edie and his family. The parents, who must have married about 1790, both died in 1839 of full age at 74 and 69. Ten children were mentioned there, three of whom died in infancy. In 1812 the seven living were aged between 20 and an infant a year old. The following year they lost their second son, David aged 16. Eight years later there was a double blow when their eldest child Elizabeth died at 29, and a younger son Arthur was lost at sea aged only 16. Four years later came another double blow when John was lost at sea aged 25, and his closest brother Alexander, a Lieutenant in the Honourable East India Company's Service died in India at 24. Only three sons out-lived the parents. Robert, the eldest followed his father in farming, removed to Abernethy and died there in 1851; Charles emigrated to Canada and the youngest, Peter died at the age of 46.

We now return to Thomas Chalmers, these two young men and the reason for the little book about them. In the spring of 1812, the newly fired minister was preaching in the parish church on that simplest summary of the Christian faith expressed in St John's

---

79 Mitchell, J. F. & S. 'Monumental Inscriptions in East Fife (before 1855)', typescript (1971) p. 187 No. 56. The stone later fell and became badly weathered. In 2008 it was restored by the family in Canada using the wording previously recorded.

14 EASTER KILMANY FARMHOUSE showing the old house on the right with the large extension of 1802.

Gospel, chapter three verse sixteen.[80] Both Alexander and Robert were in the congregation, and both dated their conversion from that day. This only drew them closer into a life-long friendship and closer to Chalmers though he only spent two more years in Kilmany. Paterson, too, was anxious to share his faith when opportunity arose. While living in a bothie at Cruivie with a ploughman whose passion was collecting ballad music, he was heard reading his Bible in the early morning. His companion asked him to read it aloud, and from that beginning the ploughman found the same faith, destroyed his ballads and instead sang the Psalms at the plough. This quiet evangelist gift led in time to Paterson, the simple ploughman of Kilmany, finding his true vocation as a Church of Scotland lay missionary among the poorest in the capital city of Edinburgh. There he worked selflessly for many years, incidentally becoming such a well-known figure. Chalmers later remarked of him that "it emphatically may be said of him that he 'Did what he could:' his labours have been more blessed than those of any man I know." He also fathered a family, one of whom became a missionary doctor in

---

80 "God so loved the world, that he gave his only begotten Son, that whosoever believeth in him, should not perish but have everlasting life."

India, and whose own son carried on his work. Four years after Chalmers, and a few months after Robert Edie, Paterson died in Edinburgh of illness contracted after ministering to a beggar suffering from typhoid.

Chalmers was gifted in many ways – scientist, philosopher and theologian, and with a great concern for the poor, but intensely practical withal. Kilmany had long had problems with the manse. James Thomsone had been non resident for want of one,[81] and whatever was then provided had become damp and unsuitable. It stood to the east of the church and you can still see the grassy path and the doorway in the wall which led to it. Chalmers thought and acted boldly. He caused the heritors to build new on a fresh site "four hundred paces" to the west. It was "in every way suitable to the accommodation of the minister" and the "ground about the manse was laid out with great taste by Dr Chalmers."[82] Thus when

15 KILMANY MANSE in 1894 and built for Chalmers in 1810. Since the Reformation provision of housing for the minister had often been an issue and sometimes lacking altogether, perhaps for the first time it was now properly supplied.

---

81 *Fasti.*
82 Cook, H. D. *op. cit.* p. 554.

Henry Cook came in 1815 he had a much better home than did his brother before 1803.

Something more can be said about the ownership of land in the parish at this time. The United College of St Andrews feued out the 4,042 acres of the parish. It was divided into fourteen estates. They varied in size from 700 down to 54, acres, though that was part of a larger holding over the parish border, and were owned by ten landed proprietors who were the heritors referred to earlier. The enclosures and improvements of 1780s and 1790s had been achieved through the draining of marshy areas and as a result any small tenant holdings were consolidated into larger farms. These were leased by tenants for nineteen year periods which could be renewed. Heritors were increasingly prosperous. The largest of these, David Gillespie of Kirkton built a spacious new country house at **Mountquhanie**, while John Anstruther Thomson of Charleton, one of the four absentee heritors, created a pleasant occasional retreat and hunting lodge called **Kilmany** Cottage which is discussed more fully later.[83] Such properties were surrounded by woods and gardens.

There are several readily available lists of the landed estates within the parish of Kilmany. Sibbald (1710) gives their names and those of the heritors. Chalmers made a return in May 1811 giving similar details together with the acreage, rental value and first year of the present 19 year lease where appropriate, with additional notes. Henry Cook (1838) has a useful discussion and Millar (1895) gives a more detailed historical summary of each of them. Chalmers lists them more or less as they lie east to west: Easter **Kinnear,** 400 acres (Kinneir of Kinloch out of the parish), Wester **Kinnear** 120 acres (Scrymgeour Wedderburn of Birkhill out of the parish), Easter **Kilmany** 292 acres, Wester **Kilmany** 342 acres and Cleughies 84½ acres (Anstruther Thomson of Charleton, out of the parish), **Newbigging** 54 acres (Mrs Robertson of Balindean which adjoined it but was out of the parish), **Rathillet** 500 acres (Carswell), **Lochmalony** and **Middlemiln** 320 acres (Mrs Scott), **Hillcarney** 256 acres (David Lawrie), **Myrecarney** 260 acres (Miss Somerville), **(Murdo)Carney** 380 acres and **Mountquhanie** 700 acres, including **Drumnod** and **Stirton** (Gillespie of Kirkton), **Starr** Farm 208 acres

---

83 Partly referred to in Cook, H. D., *op. cit.*, pp. 538 & 542; see also Leighton, *op. cit.* III, p. 58.

and the remainder of **Starr** 166 acres (Simson). Some of these estates have been mentioned already, sometimes proprietors changed after only a generation or two and were of no significance on the wider scene. Those of greater note, and often long tenure, were those who were non-resident because of landed connections outside the parish, or though resident who had wider interests elsewhere. At the end of the nineteenth century **Easter Kinnear** was held by John Boyd Kinnear of Kinloch (1828–1920). A journalist, he had been with Garibaldi and much later entered the House of Commons briefly as the Radical Unionist Member for East Fife from 1885–1886. Thereafter he returned to his Fife roots and spent the next twenty years as a hands-on improving landowner.

The Scrymgeour-Wedderburns who held **Wester Kinnear** but lived at Birkhill were Hereditary Standard Bearers for Scotland and *de jure* Earls of Dundee until this peerage was called out of abeyance in 1953 in favour of the *de facto* eleventh Earl (1902–1983). Sibbald (1710) quotes the New Valuation of Fifeshire, 1695 showing the Kilmany lands divided into three holdings, Aitherney's part, Newton's part, and Denmoor's part. Newton's part valued at £528 was the third most valuable in the parish. The grandfather of the first John Anstruther Thomson of Charleton had purchased that estate in 1713 from Colonel John Hope, and thereafter was known as John Thomson of Newton after the old house. He gave the "**Kilmeaine**" lands to a younger son, Alexander, but it was his eldest son who built the new mansion of Charleton in 1760 and renamed himself John Thomson of Charleton. Newton's part of Kilmany which is listed in the Fife Valuation of 1695 therefore presumably belonged to Colonel John Hope, then to John Thomson of Newton, then to his younger son Alexander before reverting to the Thomsons of Charleton who came to possess all three.[84]

Mountquhanie remains the principal house in the parish of Kilmany. Anciently its lands belonged to the MacDuffs, Earls of Fife. Then they passed for nearly three hundred and fifty years to the Balfour family, one of whom died at Flodden, another was involved in the murder of Cardinal Beaton (Bethune) at St Andrews, and a third served in the galleys with John Knox. In the next century

---

84   Anstruther Thomson, J. *Eighty Years' Reminiscences,* London (1904) Volume 1, p. 2 and Mitchell and Mitchell, *op. cit.* p. 176, Kilconquhar Churchyard No. 79.

Mountquhanie passed to the Lumsdens (Lumsdains). During the Civil War, Major-General Robert Lumsden, loyal to the House of Stuart, was Governor of Dundee in 1651 when it was captured and sacked by Monck. Lumsden courageously defied the roundheads from the Old Steeple of Dundee, but was treacherously executed after an honourable surrender. After some years of financial difficulty under his son it passed to a branch of the Crawfords who retained it into the eighteenth century.

By 1722 the fourth Lord Rollo was proprietor. Having been with the Jacobites at Sheriffmuir during the '15, he was imprisoned but pardoned two years later. Soon after that the estate was bought by Sir William Calderwood who became Lord Polton as a Senator of the College of Justice. With his main estate near Edinburgh, he was largely an absentee here, but on at least one occasion a meeting of the heritors was postponed because it was known that he was shortly coming to Fife. "An upright judicious dispassionate man, and never interfered in politics, which in his time had run very high" was the view of the wife of his son who after a decade succeeded him at Polton and Mountquhanie. Thomas Calderwood was "an easy-going man who later entrusted the care of his estate to his wife", Margaret, diarist and traveller. He "was a good linguist and fond of books," presenting the manuscript by an earlier member of his family to the British Museum. This was David Calderwood's 'History of the Church of Scotland'. Thomas was laird of Mountquhanie for over thirty years but the estate was sold in the mid 1760s.

Doctor John Gillespie, laird of Kirkton in Forgan became possessed of Mountquhanie and its Castle, and this would become the seat of the family which had been upwardly mobile during the previous century when a skipper in Elie had married and acquired an estate. The Doctor, who died in 1792, was succeeded by three generations, all called David, who succeeded one another for the next century.[85]

When David Gillespie (c.1770–1827) inherited the estate it was the largest in the parish of Kilmany and consisted of three farms, **Stirton, Mountquhanie and Drumnod.** The old buildings of Mountquhanie Castle, which had been augmented with seventeenth

---

85 Millar, A. H. *Fife: Pictorial and Historical,* Cupar (1895) Vol II, pp. 5 & 311–314.

century additions were abandoned as a dwelling when he built the new mansion-house (*circa* 1820) using the architect J. Gillespie Graham. The outside aspect has been described as a "long spread of a house" with a "two-storey and basement main block with a fluted parapet and Roman Doric portico." There is a "bow-ended projection at the rear of the main block's backside." The "monogrammed stone recording a charter of the lands granted in 1353" clearly refers to the confirmation by King David II (1329–71), the ineffectual son of Robert the Bruce, of the grant to the Balfours. The "single-storey and basement wings" have "pedimented centres", while "the side and rear elevations were utilitarian even before recent alterations." Access inside is through the "Grand entrance hall with a screen of scargiola Ionic columns to the imperial stair." Then on the left is the library "with a black marble console-corniced chimney piece and contemporary bookcases" with the drawing room in the west wing. An Edwardian replacement chimney piece was installed "in the bow-ended dining room behind. The main floor's

16 MOUNTQUHANIE HOUSE built below the Castle in 1820 by David Gillespie.

east side contained the principal bed and dressing rooms, with a school room (perhaps originally the billiard room) in the wing."[86]

The stables have a "front block dated 1811" and a "back range dated 1774" which "incorporates a gateway dated 1683, the entrance to the barmkiln enclosure of Mountquhanie Castle..."

Gillespie had married Mary Carnegie of the family of the Earls of Southesk (who have since become the Dukes of Fife through marrying royalty) and his daughter married another. He added the lands of Carney, Murdocairnie and Starr to his own. His son, David (1814–1899) was educated at Harrow and Christ Church, and in old age wrote of what it was like to travel from Kilmany to Oxford in 1830s before railways.

> I went up to Christ Church as a Gentleman Commoner at Easter 1833 ... travelling from my private tutor's [in] Leicester, by the "Pig and Whistle", the coach celebrated in "Tom Brown's Schooldays". ... £500 a year was a pretty usual allowance for a Gentleman Commoner, and £300 for a Commoner. ... In my time there were scarcely more than half-a-dozen Scotchmen ... whose homes were in Scotland. ... It took four days and a half hard travelling to get to Fife from Oxford by coach; three days by Dundee steamer. I took up Paddy [his hunter] ... once by land, and once by steamer. My servant ... rode him all the way by land (14 days).

He later married Susan, daughter of General Alexander Bethune of Blebo (who was born Alexander Sharp). This was in 1840, when she was only nineteen. Reputedly a great beauty, she was known as "the rose of Fife". The families of the two locally murdered Archbishops, Cardinal Beaton and James Sharp, were united in General Bethune, since his father was Sir Alexander Sharp, and his mother Margaret Bethune of Blebo the heiress through whom he inherited that estate and causing him to change his name.

Two of Gillespie's contemporaries at Christ Church became Viceroys of India, so that his life seems very pedestrian in comparison. Typical of his class, he was a Deputy Lieutenant and J.P. for the county, but his other public service was written up shortly before his death in 1899: "For length of service in the

---

86 Gifford, *op. cit.* p. 326.

government of the county no one living can compare."[87] Moreover, unlike Viceroys, it was all given voluntarily.

About 1840 he became one of the Commissioners of Supply for Fife. "Responsible for administration before the County Councils were established" these few men "conducted the public business of Fife with an efficiency, so far as the statutes empowered them, that would compare favourably with the management of the County Council, and certainly with much greater economy." As Chairman of Cupar Road Trustees from 1841–1890, he was chiefly responsible for consolidating the different turnpike road trusts into one, making large savings so that "in a few years the whole debts on the District were paid off." He also served as Chairman of the first Lunacy Board from 1858–1890. Charged with securing a site and erecting a suitable building, he engaged as architect Charles Kinnear, the brother of a fellow heritor, and as Medical Superintendent, Dr Batty Tuke (later knighted).

Greatly interested in the Volunteer Movement, he was Captain of the Cupar Corps and "what he has done for religious and philanthropic causes does not require to be related here." However, one or two may be mentioned as examples. He was a lifelong member at St James's Episcopal Church in Cupar and was prominent in wider Christian activity. In other areas he held an annual Handwriting Competition open to all for a cash prize. As a very young man he had instructed the Minister in 1837 "to give coals to every person in the parish, who I thought stood in need of them; and I was particularly requested by him, not to diminish the ordinary supply afforded to the poor, in consequence of his donation." In addition to them, "several families, who were in distress from accidental circumstances, were thus supplied."[88]

Nevertheless his main interest had been that:
> For two-thirds of a century he has borne the responsibilities and discharged the duties of a landed proprietor and country gentlemen, living on his estate and interesting himself in the welfare alike of farm tenant and humble cottar. In such a life there may not be much of

---

87 *St Andrews Citizen*, 9 June 1899, p. 8, 'Men of Fife' No. XIV: David Gillespie, Esq. of Mountquhanie.

88 Cook, H. D. *op. cit.* p. 556.

exciting interest; but it has been one full of usefulness.[89]
He may have been "a rich man in his castle" but at least he had a conscience about "the poor man at his gate." At their Golden Wedding in 1890, the couple received:

> the gifts and good wishes of a host of personal friends, the tenantry, the estate servants, Cupar Tradesmen, and the congregation of St James's. ... The address by the tenantry bore the names of seventeen tenants on Mountquhanie and Kirkton, and was adorned with views of Mountquhanie, Mountquhanie Castle, Kirkton, and Creich Castle, and was enclosed in a casket made from one of the trees more than six hundred years old which are grown on the Kirkton estate.

Despite all these possessions, the Gillespies' great tragedy was that each of their four children was childless. A stained glass window by Ballantyne of Edinburgh was erected to the couple in Creich Parish Church by their daughter and son-in-law from nearby Aytounhill. It is inscribed under the text: "Be thou faithful unto death and I will give thee a crown of life".

Then in 1904 their son David (d. 1911) sold the estate to their nephew, and his first cousin, Harry Bethune (1866–1946), another grandson of General Bethune. Colonel Bethune's only child, Mary Sharp Bethune married a Wedderburn and in that family the lands remain. They also run Mountquhanie Holiday Homes.[90]

There are other curious twists to the ownership of this place. These lands from which a Balfour set out to share in the killing of Cardinal Beaton adjoin Rathillet on the one side, whose master was convicted of the murder of Archbishop Sharp, while on the other are the lands of Creich (outside the parish of Kilmany), birthplace of Mary Bethune, one of Mary Queen of Scots' "four Maries", of the same family as the Cardinal and of the present owner's mother.

Despite his non-residence, there can be no doubt that John Anstruther Thomson, particularly after his marriage in 1807, spent much time and care on his lands at Kilmany, though at a distance of twenty miles from his home. Easter Kilmany farmhouse, was greatly

---

89 'Men of Fife' *op. cit.*
90 Gillespie, D. *Reminiscences of Christ Church, Oxford Sixty Years Ago*, privately printed (1893), pp. 5 & 16–17; Bethune, A. *Fife Sharps and Bethunes*, (1997) p. 337

enlarged in 1802, and there is further evidence of his activity.[91]

The Cook brothers bear this out in their descriptions of **Ghoules' Den** since they make a comparison between the situation there in the 1790s and the 1830s.

> Scarcely a mile to the N. of Kilmany, there is a romantic rocky den, cut deep in the face of the mountain. It has probably been gradually worn down by the successive torrents, which the heavy rains in winter throw from the higher ground, dashing amongst its rocks. The name it has received in the country is Ghoule's Den. By those who live near it, no explanation of the name is given. The manner in which it is written here would lead any one, acquainted with the Arabian Nights Entertainments, to imagine, that superstitious terrors had peopled it with the destroying demons mentioned in one of their stories. The fact is, that dismal reports, of what had been seen and heard there, were in other days circulated; reports which have had often less to gain them credit, than the dismal gloom which the shades of night must draw over that rugged unfrequented scene.[92]

Dr Cook's scepticism is not shared by the compiler of a "Tour of The Old Fermtoun of Kilmany" found on the internet in 2003, who states that "if you have the courage to venture here at the witching hour you are apt to see 'white ladies' and other shades of the departed, who found Kilmany so beautiful they haunt it yet." Cook's brother writes nearly half a century after him: "Ghouales den is the only fissure of importance in the parish. ... It was planted with great taste by the late proprietor, Mr Thomson, and beautiful walks were made through it; but these, since his lamented death, have been permitted in a degree, to go out of order."[93] The state of neglect is naturally very much greater now. Speculation on the name by which it is known must embrace the fact that "all Fife suffered in the remarkable outbreak of witchcraft that followed the Reformation" and even in the first half of the nineteenth century it could be said that "as Fife folk of the older generation still tell, witches were to be found in nearly every village until a generation or two ago, though

---

91 *Central and North Fife,* Central and North Fife Preservation Society, (1965) p. 17.

92 Cook, J. *op. cit.* pp. 424–425.

93 Cook, H.D. *op. cit.* p. 533.

their chief characteristic seems, from the stories that survive, to have been the ability to transform themselves into hares or cats."[94] Moreover

> the belief in fairies and the Gyr-Carlin (Gyre-Carling), their queen, was widespread in Fife till a century ago, and tales still linger in the remoter parts as to their doings. Will-o'-the-wisp lured to destruction fishermen off the coast as well as belated wanderers on land. Brownies helped in thrashing the corn and milking the kye; kelpies and mermaids were as often seen as are seals and otters nowadays; while bogles and ghosts haunted every lonely unhallowed spot.[95]

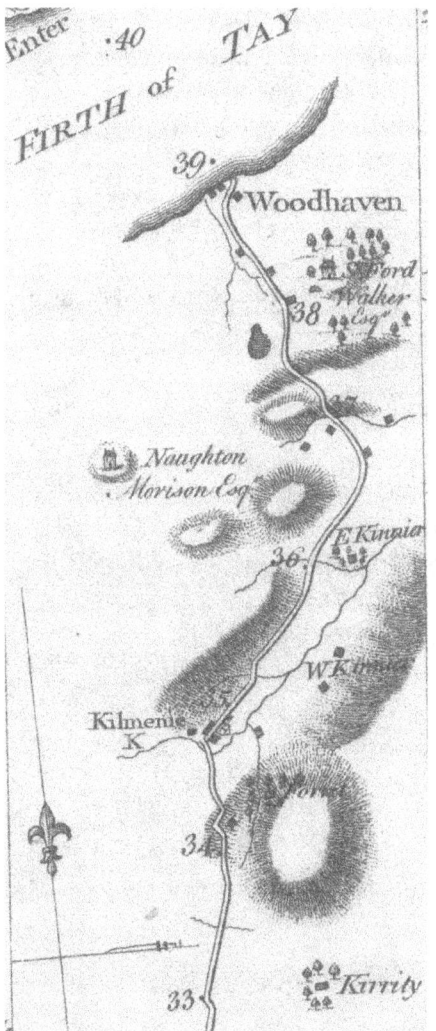

Communications were also developing apace around the beginning of the nineteenth century. John Cook noted that the effect of such changes was not wholly beneficial. Writing of household provisions, he reflects:

> It was once easy to bring, at all hours, such supplies to Kilmany; for the high road betwixt Cupar and Dundee run[s] through the village. Some years ago (for it is of late that Fife can boast of having a turnpike road), the course of this road was turned eastwards, three miles from Kilmany. The public profited by the change, for they travel by a smooth instead of a hilly road; but the village suffered; for it no longer enjoys the wonted frequent opportunities of convey-

17 COACH ROAD showing tortuous bend coming down the slope of Forret Hill avoided by the later turnpike. (Road map published by Act of Parliament 23 January 1776.)

ance betwixt Cupar and Dundee.[96]

Transport, other than one's own, remains a challenge still.

Such changes were part of even greater developments, recorded by Leighton in the 1830s. In the forenoon of 28 May 1815, a pinnace capsized on the ferry journey across the Tay to Newport. It is thought that twenty-five were on board but only seven were saved. The disaster was entirely the fault of the boatman and led to heightened concern about the safety of the ferries.[97]

> Previous to 1822, there were two ferries across the Tay, one at Newport, and one at Woodhaven, about a mile to the west; and from 1790, when a new turnpike road was made to the latter place, till 1808, it was the ferry chiefly resorted to. Another turnpike having been constructed in that year to Newport, which rendered it the most convenient point for passengers from the south, that place became in time the principal port, and the ferry at Woodhaven became much less frequented. Up to this time, the boats used were small and inconvenient, and the ferry was not always accomplished without considerable danger. In 1819, an act of parliament was obtained, by which trustees were appointed connected with the two counties of Fife and Forfar, authorising them to erect new piers, and to procure boats better fitted for the passage, and otherwise to improve and regulate the ferry. In 1822, a steam boat was placed upon the ferry, which at first plied alternately between Woodhaven and Newport; but, in 1822, the passage to Woodhaven was discontinued; after which the intercourse at the ferry began rapidly to increase.

It required an Act of Parliament to allow the Trustees to switch from one to the other.

> From being, therefore, one of the worst and most dangerous ferries, this has now become one of the most safe and convenient in the kingdom. The steam boat, however, only plies through the day; but for the convenience of the public, the trustees maintain a large sail boat, a pinnace, and a yawl, with proper crews, which may be freighted at hours when the steam boat does not

---

96 Cook, J. *op. cit.* p. 429.

97 Neish, J. S. *History of Newport and the Parish of Forgan,* Dundee (1890) pp. 29–33

ply.[98]

Anstruther Thomson (1776-1833) inherited Charleton in 1797 on the death of his mother. During the first Napoleonic scare he raised a troop of the Fife Fencible Cavalry, of which his father was Colonel, and became a Major in the Fife Yeomanry in 1800. For three years, from 1803-06 he was Master of Foxhounds from his own kennels, and thereafter his pack became the basis of the Fife Hunt. In 1807 he married Clementina Adam, whose father, the Right Honourable William Adam, M.P. of Blair-Adam, south of Kinross, was a nephew of Robert Adam the architect.[99] In the same year he succeeded to the command of the Fife Yeomanry as colonel, and the Yeomanry song, "Cornel Tamson" must date from this time. The first verse is a call to join up; the second describes the terms; the third envisages the need to serve overseas fighting "France and Flanders" and anyone else for that matter; and the fourth anticipates a safe return with "vast sums of money" and "to push about the flowing bowl".

> *We're the Light Horse of Fifeshire, sae merrily we'll go*
> *Along with Cornel Tamson, that valiant hero.*

This rousing chorus concluded each verse. It proved to be all "moonshine", of course, for Fife volunteers did not serve overseas for another ninety years when they sailed for South Africa in 1900. By then "Cornel Tamson"'s son was their honorary Colonel, though far too old for active service himself.

The first Anstruther Thomson represents the last generation to live unaffected by the railways and the greater ease of travel they provided. Forty years after his death, his widow recalled the routine of their life in Fife in a letter to her son's wife, "I had no routine more than every one must have who has a husband whose wishes she must consider, and who has a house, children and servants to look after. ..."

> After breakfast I ordered dinner, etc., etc., and John's father rode over his farm; then I possibly wrote letters or went into the garden or read my book. We rode out, or if J. was hunting, which was only twice a week, or he had gone up to one of the farms or to Cupar, I either spent my time in the garden or drove out and visited my neighbours

---

98 Leighton, *op. cit.* Vol III pp. 62–64.
99 Anstruther Thomson *op. cit.* p. 4; standard reference books.

occasionally.

> In summer evenings we used to have pleasant walks making plans for improvements. In winter read, and I worked or played on the piano. We had often the doctor or the minister or sometimes a stray man came to dinner, for in those days a man would come in or send his groom before with saddlebags and come and stay a night or two. All visitors came for a night or two, either offering to come or by invitation, but company dinners were unknown. The old Colonel and his sisters often came over from Coates, and we went there.
>
> We used to go to visit for a couple of days in the county, but there were no railroads, and few strangers came among us.

Such visits were mainly in Fife and no further than East Lothian or Perthshire. The winter of 1810 was spent in London and two later winters were spent in Edinburgh, and he went to the Highlands each year to shoot. "In '29 we went to Leamington for his health. He had always suffered much at times… and we latterly saw few people but my father, aunts and brothers, and a blessing they were to me."

This strong sense of family ties was, she believed, because

> It was always my father's desire to cherish the affection between my brothers and myself, and it has proved a comfort while they were spared, and John's father fully shared in it; and we tried to follow it out with our children, and I cannot tell you the blessing this has been to me for more than forty years now.

There were seven of these children, two boys and five girls, and clearly there had been difficult pregnancies for she "had to spend many months on the sofa before some of the children came" and "could not get out much."

Though naturally spending most of their time at Charleton, there is no doubt that during their twenty-six years of marriage, this couple spent a good deal of attention on their Kilmany estate also. Perhaps it was her artistic sensibility which inspired the planting of **Ghoule's Den**. At Kilmany there was an inn, but turn-pike developments gave advantage to another which was situated near the toll bar at Rathillet. They turned the inn into an "unpretentious house in the cottage style" as a home for casual stays. It was transformed in 1816 for Thomson by the architect Alexander Blyth, and Leighton observed that "John Anstruther Thomson, Esq. … has

18 This sylvan view of KILMANY COTTAGE was taken many years later but perhaps reflects the careful planting for which its creators were noted.

a very beautiful cottage here, near the village."[100] Her natural affection for Kilmany will become apparent later.

Something of the elegance of the man, and of the age, is shown in a letter which he wrote to Chalmers on hearing of the death of a Kilmany parishioner. It is dated from "Charleton, May 28, 1814 by Windygates and Colinsburgh.

> Dear Sir,
>
> Owing to the extreme irregularity of the cross-post, I did not receive your letter informing of the death of poor Mr Bonthron till the day of the funeral.
>
> It is a great satisfaction to think that by the kind interest which you took in alleviating the distress of the latter years of this unfortunate but deserving man, he has glided into the other world with composure and resignation.
>
> That everything good may affect you and your family is the sincere wish of, dear Sir, your most obedient servant,
>
> J. A. Thomson

The couple's eldest son, also John, quotes an incident which apparently took place in the summer holidays of 1827. He had

---

100 Gifford, *op. cit.* p.26, and Leighton, *op. cit.* III p. 58.

come with his father to go "out hunting with Stewart's harriers to hunt roedeer at Cruivie near Kilmany" during which there was an accident. The father sent for his wife from Charleton:

> My Dearest Clem,
>
> A horse has kicked John on the leg. It is merely a bruise, but painful. Mrs Gillespie and Tom Loch have bathed the leg in warm water and are putting leeches on it and then a poultice. It is now only about an hour since it happened, and he desires me to say to you that he has now no pain.
>
> Mrs Gillespie and Tom do not think it even necessary to send for a doctor, but I doubt he will not be able to be moved by the steam-boat on Saturday, and I think it better that you should come here, as he will be better in the carriage than a gig tomorrow.
>
> He is now asleep, and by the time that you read this I have no doubt but that he will be quite well.
>
> This house is full of ladies - Mrs Bruce, Mrs Maitland, Norah Loch and Susan Gillespie - so you see that John's hurt is not of consequence.
>
> Ever my dearest,
> Yours J. A. T.
> Kilmany, half-past Twelve, Wednesday
>
> Since writing this I have found him laughing and eating grapes, so don't come, but send the carriage to-night to take him home tomorrow morning, as it is best not to trust to the gig in case of rain.[101]

Today it is not without interest that Henry Cook tells us that "the roedeer was for long time banished from this part of the country, but of late has again made its appearance".[102] Some today will think that the Anstruther Thomsons and their friends were doing their best to extinguish it again!

The first edition of the Ordinance Survey map 1:10,560 was surveyed in 1854. Within **Ghoules' Den** "Sir Walter Scott's Tree" is marked on the western slope not far from the stream. It may well be asked what likelihood is there that Scott ever frequented this rather remote part of the parish. In fact the Anstruther Thomsons had come to know him through her father, William Adam, who had a house in

---

101 Anstruther Thomson, *op. cit.* I, pp. 8–9; Stewart, laird of St Fort.
102 Cook, H. D. *op. cit.* p. 537.

Edinburgh. Annually from 1817 to 1830 at the Summer solstice the Blair-Adam Antiquarian Club gathered, usually at Adam's country home. Never numbering more than about ten men, these included Scott, Adam and his son-in-law from Charleton.[103] In the Summer of 1827 Thomson visited Abbotsford and Scott referred to his guest in his diary: "my visitor is a country gentleman of the best description. Knows the world having been a good deal attached both to the turf and the field is extremely good humoured and a good deal of a local antiquary. I showed him the plantations."[104] When Thomson left for Minto the following day Scott observed: "parting a pleased guest I hope from a pleased landlord. When I see a ge'man is a ge'man as the blackguards say, why I know how to be civil."[105] In June of that same year the Club met at Charleton and unusually not at Blair-Adam. Again Scott's diary records the event:

> Our good-natured host, Mr A. Thompson, his wife and his good-looking daughters, received us most kindly and the conversation took its old roll in spite of woes and infirmities. Charlton is a good house in the midst of highly cultivated land and immediately surround[ed] with gar[d]ens and parterres together with plantations, partly in the old partly in the new taste. I like it very much though as a residence it is perhaps a little too much finished. Not even a bit of bog to amuse one, as Mr El[p]hinstone said.[106]

and though they visited St Andrews they did not come in the Kilmany direction.[107]

However, there is another source than Scott's diary from which we know that there was an earlier meeting of the Blair-Adam Club which did include a visit to Kilmany. This may explain what would otherwise be a mystery. William Adam printed his *Remarks on The Blair-Adam Estate* in 1834. This was the year after Anstruther

---

103 Anderson, W. E. K. *Sir Walter Scott's Journal*, Oxford (1972), Introduction p. xxxv. The usual spelling is *Charleton* rather than *Charlton*.

104 *Ibid.*, (Tuesday, 27 March 1827).

105 *Ibid.*, p.292 (Wednesday, 28 March 1827).

106 *Ibid.*, p. 315 (15 June 1827).

107 Scott's visit to Charleton lasted only from 15–18 June 1827. On the 16th their excursion took them to St Andrews, and the 17th was spent more locally. They cannot have come to Kilmany on this visit.

Thomson had died at the age of 56, and two years after Scott's death. Adam greatly lamented the passing of both, and described Thomson as "one I loved so much for his virtues" and having "a kind heart, an excellent understanding, exemplary virtues, and the principles of pure religion, [which] directed him in the performance of all his duties."[108]

Without giving dates he mentioned two separate years when the Club met at Charleton, and clearly that in 1827 referred to above was the second, (and Scott's Journal did not commence until 1825.) Included in the company on the first occasion was Sir Henry Raeburn, who died in 1823. After a visit to Magus Muir, he then refers to "Mr Thomson's beautiful cottage at **Kilmainey,** where we had repast, rather more urbane than that at the Trafalgar Inn, but not less joyous."[109] It was presumably on this earlier occasion that the party walked in the Den and the tree may very well have been named by Scott on this occasion. The story is that while the party were walking in the plantations recently laid out, Scott called out, "This is my tree" as he struck one of them.[110]

Thomson's heir was a fifteen year old schoolboy at Eton. The new laird soon became a soldier but was above all committed to fox hunting. In 1847 he sent in his papers to become a Master of Fox Hounds, and entered more actively into possession of the Charleton and Kilmany estates. However, for many years to come he continued to spend long months of most years away from home hunting.

He was Master of Foxhounds in Fife for twenty-one years (1849–50, 1858–64, and 1873–88), and for fifteen years elsewhere (The Atherstone, 1847–49, 1850-55, 1870–71; The Bicester 1855–57; and The Pytchley 1864–69). Those in England meant that he was away from Fife from early Autumn to late Spring, and even when not in an official capacity he made long hunting tours into other parts of the British Isles as well as family trips to Europe. In November 1895 he was in the Cotswolds reminiscing with a group of friends when one picked up a list of hunts and they went through it to see how many each one of them had ever been out with. His

---

108 Anderson *op. cit.*, pp. xiv & xvi.

109 *Ibid.*, p. xxii

110 *Ibid.*, p. xxii. The tree has long since been blown down.

own score of 101 greatly exceeded anyone else's and ranged from the North of Scotland to Cornwall and from East Anglia to Ireland. In 1860 he was active in raising afresh the Fife Light Horse volunteers; from 1865-95 he was their commanding officer, and thereafter honorary Colonel. As a result of this, and unlike his father, he could not be frequently about his farms, and no doubt his factor was a key figure therein. Nevertheless he seems to have been personally popular, and was inevitably celebrated in the songs of volunteers and huntsmen. Here is one anonymous example:

> *Who sprang to lift me when I fell*
> *And heaved my sheltie up as well?*
> *That Devon common drain could tell –*
>
> *Jack Thomson.*
>
> *Who hunts upon the edge of frost*
> *Rather than let a day be lost?*
> *Ae man, but in himself a host –*
>
> *Jack Thomson.*
>
> *Who rides the country up and down,*
> *With smile like morn for peer and clown?*
> *Most genial lad beneath the crown –*
>
> *Jack Thomson.*
>
> *Who makes the shire one family –*
> *A freen to all in each degree –*
> *Gars Whig and Tory brithers be?*
>
> *Jack Thomson.*
>
> *"John Thomson's bairns" means easy free –*
> *Auld Fife phrase for guid company –*
> *Our common father yet is he –*
>
> *John Thomson.*

As for **Kilmany** during this period, his widowed mother outlived her husband by the best part of half a century, and as early as January 1844 her son spent his leave at Kilmany where his mother was living. Clearly she came to use the "Kilmany Cottage" as her country home, more particularly perhaps after his marriage in 1852 having also a house in London. The residents' list of 1862 includes "Mrs & Misses Thomson" residing here, for of the "good looking daughters" two never married.[111]

---

111 Westwood, A. (publisher) *Parochial Directory of Fife and Kinross Shires*, Cupar (1862) p.128.

19 IMPROVEMENTS IN HOUSING

Late eighteenth century improvements in agriculture and greater prosperity led to better housing being provided and not only for the lairds. The cottages of estate workers were built up to include larger windows, more space and less overcrowding, often, as here, with garret rooms above, providing a considerable advance on the "straggling huts" described in the 1790s. In this impression, the cottages on the west side of the Church are shown as they may have been about 1835. The thatch was not replaced by pantiles until later in the century, and indoor sanitation was delayed until well after a new century had dawned. Here two bothies constructed against the front of the building provided sleeping accommodation for apprentices at the Smithy opposite, or for extra hands at Easter Kilmany farm.

A few individuals were upwardly mobile too. Of three generations of the Pryde family, the first two practised their shoemaking trade here throughout most of the nineteenth century, while the third won his way through Madras College and the University, two levels of education unknown to his forebears, into the Church of Scotland ministry.

When the elder Cook told us that all the parishioners were occupied in agriculture he was not denying the existence of the miller and smith, for they too were wholly dependent on agriculture. The younger Cook is more explicit (1838). "What is called the village of Kilmany consists of the cottar's houses of the two farms of the same name, with those of the wright, smith, shoesmith, weaver, and beadle; and of a few more families."[112] Then in greater detail:

---

112 Cook, H. D. *op. cit.* p. 552.

The number of males employed in agriculture is 120. They may thus be divided: proprietors farming their estates or part of them, 5; tenants, 12; cottars or agricultural married servants, 37; unmarried do., 66; total, 120. The industry of the parish in other respects may be estimated from the following statement: day labourers, 18; weavers, 10; wrights, 2 masters, workmen and apprentices, 11; sawyers, 5; smiths, 6 masters, workmen and apprentices, 4; publican, 1; toll-keeper, 1; tailors, 2 masters, apprentices, 1; masons, 3; gardeners, 2 masters, workmen and apprentices, 4; grocers in a small way, 2; millers, 3, assistants etc, 3; beadle, 1; shoemakers, 3 masters, workmen and apprentices, 6; ministers, 1 Established, 1 Secession; parochial schoolmaster 1, schoolmistresses, 2; butler, gamekeeper etc, 5; retired 3; total, 101.

There is no large manufactory in the parish. The weavers are employed in home work, and when this cannot be obtained, they are supplied with Osnaburgh, or other cloth, by the merchants of Dundee and Cupar; or by their agents in the country. In addition to the number who weave, mentioned above, there are several females who occupy themselves in this manner, during the winter. In

20 KILMANY SAWMILL in 1894. In front of this on the left of the road the Public Baths were later built, and the statue of Jim Clark is now located there. The buildings behind became the Dairy after the Sawmill closed.

> summer, they generally give up this work when the farmers need their assistance.
>
> The only branch of industry, except agriculture, which is carried on to any extent, is the saw-mill, which was some years ago erected by Mr Thomson of Charleton. It has been occupied ever since it was built, by Mr William Malcolm, wright. During the course of the year, it is by him actively employed, and cuts down a considerable quantity of wood. Its power is not sufficiently strong for large trees, but it is admirably adapted for cutting paling, for preparing wood for sheep flakes, and for converting inferior timber into staves for herring barrels. Many hundreds of these are annually sent from this mill to Leith, and other places on the Forth where herrings are cured.[113]

He also tells us that 'the population of Kilmany has been decreasing for many years." This was due both to the increasing mechanisation of farming and to the pull of the new industries in the towns.

> This arises from the enlargement of the farms, from the want of ground for feuing, and from the introduction of machinery for bodily and manual labour. ... From the time when the last Statistical Account was written, thrashing-mills have been universally introduced, and have led to a considerable diminution of the population; and individuals with large families naturally retire from a parish, where there are no manufactories, to towns and places where they can obtain employment for their children.[114]

In 1762 a dissenting church (similar to the Established but opposed to links with the state) had been started at Rathillet owing to the unpopularity of the newly appointed Kilmany minister, William Gibb, who in fact only stayed for two years. As the only such church in the area, this drew people from a wide area. The 1947 *Statistical Account* noted "traces of kirk roads to Rathillet from Logie, Gauldry, Brunton, etc." After the Disruption within the established Church in 1843 there were inevitably further ramifications for congregations in the locality. When withdrawing from active politics after the Parliamentary election in 1864, Anstruther Thomson wrote to his father-in-law the Revd Mr Gray,

---

113 *Ibid*, p. 546.
114 *Ibid*, pp. 544–545.

21 THE UNITED PRESBYTERIAN CHURCH AT RATHILLET. Founded in 1762, the congregation worshiped in a simple, barn-like building for nearly a hundred years. A decent manse was provided in 1849. This was followed in 1859 with ambitious plans for a new church, designed by the Dundee architects, Edward and Robertson. James Miller, tenant farmer at Easter Kinnear, provided half the cost. After Reunion of Scottish Presbyterians in 1929, it was anomalous to have two churches in Kilmany under the same minister. This building was only closed and demolished to allow the A92 to be diverted from the hamlet of Rathillet in the early 1960s.

landowner and parson, including this comment when discussing aspects of the election campaign:

> As to the Kilmany Free Church, it was a case of aggression on their part. There was one member of their congregation in the village of Kilmany, ninety in the village of Gauldry, and ninety in the village of Logie, where the Free Church is situated. They wished to pull down the church at Logie and put it up near Kilmany, so that 180 would have to walk one and a half miles to meet one member. I offered them a site at Gauldry, but that would not suit them. Any impartial person can judge how reasonable their request was.[115]

Like most such matters, it was not quite as simple as that. Melville, the minister at Logie, had gone over to the Free Church in 1843. He lost his church, but a new one had been built by January 1844. He lost the fine manse (which is now Lucklaw House), but a new one

---

115 Anstruther Thomson, *op. cit.* vol. 1 p. 303.

was provided by 1846 (now Ardlogie). Gauldry had no church of its own, but the Free Church opened a "station" there in 1843. When Melville died in 1848, Logie and Gauldry were united with the recommendation that a church be built at a site convenient to both. Hence the desire for a church building placed between the two villages, e.g. at Kilmany. When Anstruther Thomson refused permission, a weaver's shop in Gauldry was converted into a church in 1867. With embellishments, this is now the parish church. In time the majority of the congregation was centred there, and the Free Church at Logie was closed in 1900. We have already seen that the whole of this rural area was losing population as a result of agricultural change and "the district never recovered from the extinction of the hand loom weaving."[116]

In 1870, a poem was published entitled "the Bapteesement of the Bairn". It had been written by Robert Leighton, who died in early middle age the previous year, but too late to be included in his *Poems* of 1866. It is "not only a droll tale but also a shrewd criticism of Scottish Calvinistic narrowness."[117] Of the twenty-four lines only those leading to the conclusion concern us here:

>And what can we expect but sin and woe,
>When manses are the hotbeds where they grow?
>I grieve for puir Kilmany, and I grieve
>For Leuchars and for Forgan – yea believe
>For Soddom and Gomorrah there will be
>A better chance than ony of the three.
>Especially Kilmany, I maintain –
>For a' your reasons, sacred and profane.
>The minister that plays the fiddle's waur
>Than either o' the ither twa, by far.
>And yet, weak woman, ye wad e'en return
>And get this fiddler to bapteese our bairn.
>Na, na; we'll tak the bairn to whence it came,
>And get our ain brave minister at hame.

Despite his birth in Dundee, Leighton had been living in England for many years when he wrote. Nevertheless, as a teenager he had lived for a time at the farm of Easter Friarton close to the old church of Forgan. It is hard to know whether any of the poem is based on the

---

116 Ewing, W. *Annals of the Free Church of Scotland, 1843-1900,* Edinburgh, (1914), II, p. 149.

117 *Dictionary of National Biography*, (reprint 1959-1960) Vol. XI, p.886.

clerical personalities of the day, though the parishes of Leuchars and Kilmany adjoin that of Forgan in this North East corner of Fife.

Let us assume that "the minister that plays the fiddle" does not have a literal meaning, but simply means nonsensical trifling. Kilmany Manse was occupied for forty years from 1858 by The Revd David Brewster (1833-98) who came from an impeccably academic family, and he himself was made a Doctor of Divinity by his University of St Andrews in 1896 after many years as Clerk to the Cupar Presbytery and to the Synod of Fife. Although a noted church lawyer, "geniality and wit were his characteristics. As a singer, and lover of music, too, he was justly celebrated."[118]

Though Brewster was incumbent when Leighton wrote, his predecessor Henry Cook was a good candidate for some Calvinistic opposition. One of his brothers, George succeeded Chalmers as

22 DAVID BREWSTER was nephew of Sir David Brewster, Principal of the University of St Andrews, and he is the only Minister commemorated inside the Church by parishioners and friends.

---

118 Obituary in *Fife News*, 22 January 1898.

Professor of Moral Philosophy at St Andrews in 1829. He had been Moderator of the General Assembly in 1825, and from 1833 he was the leader of the moderate party in the Patronage question which finally split the church ten years later. Such speculations about the Kilmany minister may be irrelevant. Perhaps Leighton was not concerned with any literal reference to personalities, but simply setting his satire in a locality he had known of old.

The residents' lists of 1862 give us more details of the inhabitants.[119] Of the four blacksmiths (at Hazelton Walls, Kilmany, Knowehead and Milndeans either side of Rathillet), John Wilson was at Kilmany itself. His family provided five generations of smiths in the house between 1803 and about 1970 (ending with the widow of the last), and his descendants continue beyond Lucklaw in Balmullo (David Wilson world champion smith in 1985).[120] Of the boot and shoemakers, Jimmy Pryde carried on his trade in the bothy by the churchyard path. David Brewster (large marble monument in the church) was in the manse. Of the two farms in the village, Easter Kilmany was tenanted by William Aitken, and Wester Kilmany (where the racing driver Jim Clark was born in 1936) by George Watt; his granddaughter, who grew up there, still came out by taxi from Cupar to church every Sunday well into the 1970s. Kilmany also sported a grocer, John Lumsden, possibly the last shop-keeper apart from the post office of which he became the first master. There is an interesting note, though, that "walking postmen leave the Office at Cupar about 9.20.a.m., by the roads leading by Foodieash to Kilmany, and by Hillcairnie to Rathillet, and both return in time for the afternoon's earliest despatch."

The miller, of corn and barley, was William Wilson, while the sawmill, started by the first Anstruther Thomson, was now in the hands of Allen Law, who also carried on the trade of joiner and wright. Miss Macfarlane ran the Female Industrial School at Kilmany, while the Parish School at Rathillet (there from the 1600s until 2009) was in the hands of William M'Gillivray who was also Registrar and Session Clerk. Many of these are commemorated in the churchyard. Apart from John Rodger who kept the Anstruther

---

119 Westwood, *op. cit*. There was a fifth smith at Streetford on the Cupar road into the 1840s (Census).

120 Personal knowledge; local press reports.

Thomson's garden, the rest of those who lived and worked around the village would have been cottars or labourers.[121]

Recently it has been said that "the farmer's wife used to have her own income from the scratching corn-yard hens. And the ploo'mans wife fed two pigs a year in the stone-built pan-tiled pigsty called the pig's crave. Each farm toon had a row of 'cotton' –

23 KILMANY FLOUR MILL about 1910. The water wheel can be seen on the gable wall.

---

121 For Anstruther Thomson and Anstruther-Gray families, see *Burke's Landed Gentry*.

the cottages – every one with a perfectly kept vegetable garden at the bottom of which was a crave, an ash midden, and a dry toilet for the use of females only!"[122]

Kilmany was never simply a 'farm toon', because of its church, smithy, school and sawmill. Nevertheless these same elements will have been true of the environs of Easter and Wester Kilmany farmhouses, the former being located with its steadings and cottages spilling out around the church and smithy. A photograph of 1885 shows the view down past the smithy towards the school. A stone-built pan-tiled pig's crave is clearly visible on what is still a triangle of grass at the entry to The Wynd. We have read of the cottage gardens in Alexander Paterson's time, and evidence of a dry toilet could still be found behind the cottages next to the church path as late as the 1960s.

Three local victims of the Tay Bridge disaster of 1879 were buried here, while the name of a fourth, whose body was never found, was inscribed on the family tombstone.[123] Two of them were

24 KILMANY SMITHY in 1885. Such as it is, this lane is the main street in the hamlet, leading from the Motray bridge to the church. The work of the smith sprawls all around him. The school is at the end of the lane on the left.

---

122 Omand, *op. cit*. p. 168.
123 Neish, *op. cit.* p.216 claims five.

young men aged twenty years of age, now working as masons on the new Dundee Asylum there.

> Between David Cunningham and Robert Fowlis there was no thought of bereavement, of weariness, of anything but the great pleasure they found in each other's company. They had been friends since childhood. They lodged together at the same boarding house in Dundee, and there was little in their happily ordinary lives that these young men did not do together, from working to playing, except fall in love. Robert Fowlis was in love. In his jacket was letter from his sweetheart.[124]

William McGonagall, the tragic late nineteenth century Dundonian who believed himself to be a great poet, wrote about the Tay Bridge before and after the disaster. He also wrote about "Bonnie Kilmany". When I read all the verses to Mrs Brown at the Post Office during the 1970s she, born in 1889 and no doubt recalling her early days, remarked, "Aye, Kilmany's all there, it's all there" in a way that was no longer so, as we shall see. His efforts are worth repeating now, despite the awfulness of the rhymes, and the blindingly obvious evocation of a loveliness which we still experience – and not only in summer.

> *Bonnie Kilmany, in the county of Fife,*
> *Is a healthy spot to reside in to lengthen one's life.*
> *The scenery there in summer time is truly grand,*
> *Especially the beautiful hills and the woodland.*
>
> *And the little village in the Howe is lovely to see,*
> *In the midst of green trees and shrubbery;*
> *And the little rivulet, as it wimples along,*
> *Can be heard singing aloud an aquatic song.*
>
> *And the old church there is built on a knoll,*
> *And on the Sabbath mornings the church bell does toll,*
> *Inviting the people to join in prayer,*
> *While echoes of the bell is heard in mid-air.*
>
> *Then there's a little schoolroom, surrounded by trees,*
> *A favourite haunt for butterflies and busy bees.*
> *And an old red-tiled smithy near by,*
> *And the clink of the hammers can be heard sounding high.*

---

124 Prebble, J. *The High Girders*, London (1956) Penguin Edition (1979) p. 125.

> And there's a wood sawmill by the roadway.
> And the noise can be heard by night and day,
> As the circular saw wheels round and round,
> Making the village with its echoes resound.
>
> And in the harvest time on a fine summer morn
> The Howe looks most beautiful when the corn is shorn;
> And to hear the beautiful lark singing on high
> Will make you exclaim, "Dull care, good-bye."[125]

A chorus, repeated between each verse, need only be given here once:

> Then, bonnie Annie, will you go with me
> And leave the crowded city of Dundee,
> And breathe the pure, fragrant air
> In the Howe of Kilmany, so lovely and fair?

Rather more literary are these lines by a seven year old pupil at Kilmany School in 1973.

THE MOTRAY WATER

> The burn ripples and splashes
> as it runs over the stones.
> It rushes and gushes and sleeps
> as it slowly slithers down to the sea.
> On a moonlit night it reflects the trees.
> It is transparent.
>
> When I looked into the Kilmany burn
> I could see stones.
> The trees and the bridges
> arch over the stream.
> Transparent, on a moonlit night
> it reflects the trees.[126]

The attractiveness of Kilmany is also shown by J. S. Neish in 1890 devoting no less than twenty pages at the end of his *History of Newport* to describing a half-holiday excursion there because "to those in quest of a peaceful retreat during the summer months no better spot could be found."[127] He refers to the precentor's chair in

---

125 McGonagall, W. T. *More Poetic Gems,* pp.75-76, bound up with *Collected Poems* and *Last Poetic Gems* and reprinted in Edinburgh (1992).

126 Richard Weekes.

127 Neish, *op. cit.* p. 224.

25 KILMANY CHURCH 1894 as McGonagall will have seen it. The Lochmalony graves were then shielded by iron railings. The entrance door of the porch was soon to be moved to the opposite side to allow for a new heating boiler which required a chimney, long since taken down.

26 THE SMITHY in 1894 with Mr and Mrs Wilson standing on the cartwright's wheel on which the metal rims were heated and then shrunk onto wooden wheels, such as those stacked ready nearby.

the church, presented by Mr Horsburgh of **Lochmalony** (but since lost), which was reputedly from the home of Alexander Henderson, the minister of Leuchars already referred to. There are also some anecdotes of Chalmers, and the description of the burial of the infant of a wandering tinker: "here was a romance of gipsy life, a birth and a death in a smithy, a waif by the wayside cast on the charity and hospitality of the humble villagers."[128] The baby was born on straw in the smithy and the bereft mother taken in to be nursed by a cottager.

During the nineteenth century a number of voluntary societies sprang up in the parish. Chalmers began the Kilmany Bible Society in which subscribers committed to paying a penny a week to the British & Foreign Bible Society to provide Bibles in many languages and in many parts of the world. The heritors opposed the scheme on the grounds that it was too great a commitment for working families to make. In response it was objected they did not have a monopoly in philanthropy; the poor could make a free-will offering if they chose to do so. The society flourished over many years though not without a break. Later support came from wider sources, including the dissenters at Rathillet.

Of a totally different nature was the Rathillet Cow Society. It was inaugurated in May 1864 by nine men and continued over a number of years on a weekly basis. Reconstituted annually, the minute of 1868 states that "at a meeting in the School it was resolved to form a Cow Assurance Society for mutual help in the even of any deaths among the cows of those who become members." The premium sounds quite high, set at "entry money for each cow £1.12.4¾d, and 1/- as a quarterly payment." The assurance provided was "that £7 be paid by the Society to any member on the death of a cow which has been duly entered in the Society's books." The members were not farmers, but others, among them Allan Law of Kilmany sawmill, who probably kept a single animal. The Kilmany Curling Club was also active over a number of years, its meetings being advertised in the local press.

Earlier in the century Female Industrial Schools, to teach practical skills had been founded at Hazelton Walls by Gillespies and in Kilmany by Anthruther Thomsons. The last quarter of the

---

128 *Ibid.*, p. 214.

27 KILMANY SCHOOL in 1894. Originally built privately as a Female Industrial School, after 1873 it became a County primary school.

28 KILMANY SCHOOL CHILDREN posing outside the Post Office in 1894. Margaret Duncan (later Mrs Brown) may be among the youngest there.

nineteenth century was a time of rapidly increased mechanisation and social change; but for Kilmany village we shall see that the biggest upheaval was to come at the end of it. Old Mrs Anstruther Thomson lived to be over ninety and died at her London home in 1877. Two of her daughters lived on into the 1890s and the laird their brother until 1904, always the fox hunting man and Colonel of Volunteers. After some years as a widower, he married again in 1891 and his youngest child was born in the following year.

Vanity Fair was a weekly society magazine founded in 1868 and soon became very successful. A particular feature

29 "FIFE". Colonel Anstruther Thomson, 1882 in *Vanity Fair*.

30 KILMANY COTTAGE in 1894 leased to Colonel Conyngham McAlpine. Note that only the main block was retained in the later rebuilding (see illustration 31).

of each edition was a cartoon in colour under headings such as "Statesmen", "Men of the Day", etc. Advances in the technical development of lithography and printing led to high quality productions undertaken by the most expensive printers of the time, Vincent Brooks, Day. Originally intended as caricatures, appearance in the series soon became regarded as a social accolade. Described as "Fife" Anstruther Thomson appeared on 17 June 1882. (His son, Charlie, followed in a later edition.) Several artists were employed under pseudonyms. The most famous was "Spy", (Sir Leslie Ward), who did this one. About this time Thomson published *The History of the Fife Light Horse* (1892) which was based on a series of articles in the *Fife Journal*. Then at the age of eighty-five he told King Edward VII that he was still hunting, and had complete his two volume *Eighty Years' Reminiscences* which was published in 1904. He died that year.

Well before his death the Kilmany estate passed to his younger son, William, also heir to his mother's lands of Carntyne in Lanarkshire, who took the name of Anstruther-Gray in lieu of Thomson when he inherited in 1904. Having grown up at Charleton, and following the family tradition at Eton, he trained under his father in the Fife Light Horse. Having been commissioned into the

31 KILMANY HOUSE, built on either side of Kilmany Cottage by the architect Reginald Fairlie between 1914–1927. The cottage was adapted but can be clearly recognised between the octagonal extension and the gabled front of the new main block.

13th Hussars, he straightaway saw service in India and Afghanistan in 1880-81 before transferring into The Royal Horse Guards in 1885. His father's cousin, Sir Henry (later Lord) Loch was Governor of Victoria, and doubtless through that connection he became an A. D. C. to the Governor of South Australia, the Earl of Kintore, returning with his young bride in 1891. As a younger son he had already been greatly provided for when his father, at the age of seventy made over to him the Kilmany estate. Kilmany Cottage had been let in the 1880s first to H. D. Bell, Esq. and then to Colonel Conyngham McAlpine. The lease of 1887 was signed by John Anstruther Thomson, as proprietor, but when a variation of lease on one of the Kilmany farms was required in the following year, the factor acted for Captain William Anstruther-Thomson as proprietor, with his father acting as witness. Though now the owner of the Kilmany estate, he did not yet settle here, but after touring the world with his young wife in 1893 he continued in the army until he retired after serving in the South African War. He was at first Commandant of a District, which led to the presentation of an inscribed silver tray, and then Inspector of Concentration Camps in the Transvaal. Settling at Kilmany, he first set about entering Parliament contesting St Andrews Burghs unsuccessfully as a Unionist (Conservative) in 1903. This was in the days when Cupar and St Andrews were linked with the coastal burghs to form a constituency. He collected antiques and curiosities and also began to plan the development of his home.

When Easter Kilmany farm was leased to a new tenant in 1909, he had reserved the right to make a new road through the farm. In so doing he was able to re-route the main road away from his house (still seen from the line of the hedgerow on the A92). After the First World War he laid

32 NEW ROAD by Colonel Anstruther-Gray diverted traffic away to the back of Easter Kilmany farm (signed).

out the grounds, improved the cottages in the village, turned Jimmy Pryde's old home into his laundry and the workshop into a "museum" to house his trophies and souvenirs brought home from abroad. In 1906, William Anstruther-Gray was returned as Member of Parliament for the constituency of St Andrews Burghs,[129] which he had previously contested, a surprising achievement in an Election which nationally gave the Liberals a landslide victory. Almost inevitably he lost the seat at the January 1910 Election but won it back at the end of the year.

A Directory for 1911 shows that the Chairman of the Parish Council was Walter Marshall, J.P. of Lochmalony. There was a Post and Telegraph Office at Kilmany which did not deal with money orders, kept by Nathan Duncan who was also Registrar of Births, Marriages and Deaths. There was a lesser facility at Rathillet where Mary Menzies was sub-postmistress and later

33 ROBERT GRIEVE (under-gardener) and his wife, ELIZABETH (in her apron as the only laundry woman) outside the garden side of what is now Loaning Hill in the 1920s.

34 KILMANY LETTER BOX. Traditionally there was no red pillar box in Kilmany. A slot in a window of the Post Office served. It was a marvellous arrangement with letters dropping onto the broad wooden counter and then swept from there into a waiting post bag.

---

129 *Who Was Who*; relevant dates of *The Times*.

another at Hazelton Walls. The Inspector of the Poor also lived there, his wife being the Schoolmistress. That village also had the United Free Church minister, the Revd A. C. Dawson, and a joiner, Alexander Carmichael. There were black-smiths at Hazelton, Knowehead and Kilmany where the Wilsons continued to thrive. Also in the village was the Church of Scotland Minister, the Revd R.T. Marshall, while William Law ran the sawmill and was a joiner as well. Of the eighteen farmers listed, Thomas Miller was now tenant at Easter Kilmany and the Watt family continued at Wester Kilmany which was now farmed by Frank.

From 1914 the laird greatly expanded Kilmany Cottage into a

35 KILMANY SMITHY COMPLEX

This photograph of 1894 shows the Smithy house on the left, next to the Smith's workshop, and then the store and stable with its distinctive pointed roof. The house was given an unsightly second storey in the 1920s. The stable provided an attractive feature into the third millennium until, after long disuse, it collapsed during a storm.

The Wilson family worked the Smithy for five generations from 1803 until 1958. The buildings being too small for present needs, the sixth generation removed to nearby Balmullo where the long tradition is still being carried on. Here there was a common purpose to keep them, but it was unusual for working families to stay for generations. The twice yearly hirings in Cupar meant that the majority, who all worked on the land, were likely to move around as opportunity provided. All were dependent on the laird for their housing in this totally feudal world. The Smithy is currently being restored as a house.

large country house in which he could entertain, employing Reginald Fairlie to re-create Kilmany House as an "agreeably rambling and pantiled villa." During the First World War he returned to the army and was promoted to Lieutenant-Colonel in 1916, commanding the 3rd line Group of The Scottish Horse. The major extension of the Kilmany House was completed in 1919.

> Fairlie's client ... demanded a South African look, so on the main (garden) front Fairlie provided elaborate wrought-iron wall-ties, green shutters and pair of Cape Dutch gables with a *stoep* to their south. At the south-west corner, octagonal two storey pavilion of 1927 (by Fairlie again), making a happy stop to this elevation. Inside a corridor running the full length of the house designed to show off the owner's collection of armour. In the panelled dining room of 1927, a chimney-piece, probably seventeenth century, from a demolished house in Crail.[130]

This was the hey-day of Kilmany as a political and social centre, and since 1909 the Newburgh and North Fife railway, with a station at Kilmany, had aided better communications, as did the development of motor transport. Life in the village had been improved by provision of public baths beside the old sawmill and pigeon lofts became popular.

Though remembered as a good local member, Colonel Anstruther-Gray did not really enjoy London and left Parliament in 1918 when the seat expanded again to become North East Fife. He was a County Councillor for the Leuchars area for fourteen years until 1929, also a J.P., a deputy lieutenant for Fife, and a member of the Cupar District Council until the end of his life. He also continued to pursue an inherited love of foxhunting with the Fife Hunt, and to collect curios, a notable one being the red hat of the Cardinal Archbishop of York, brother of the Young Pretender. During the inter-war years his wife was also very active, and with the greater emancipation of women Mrs Anstruther-Gray became the first woman J.P. in Scotland. She was also a prime mover in the Scottish Women's Rural Institute, and the Kilmany branch was one of the earliest to be founded. Becoming Chairman of its central Council three years after it began, she continued in that post until 1933, and in the following year was appointed a Commander of the

---

130 Gifford, J. *op. cit.* p. 262.

36 KILMANY STATION in 1960

37 THE LOCOMOTIVE at the same time

38 OIL LAMP at St Fort Station on the Kilmany Parish boundary. This was on the mainline north. The Edinburgh and Northern Railway ran across the Forth ferry to Burntisland on to Perth (via Ladybank) and by the ferry from Tayport to Broughty Ferry on to Dundee and Aberdeen. This line commenced fully in 1850, but St Fort was probably opened in May 1848, providing the parish with its first modern transport link with the wider world. It was acquired by the North British in 1862 and through the L.N.E.R. and British Railways finally closed in September 1965.

39 ST FORT STATION looking south (1960). From the farther platform local victims of the Tay Rail Bridge disaster (1879) boarded the train. In those days this was the last stop before Dundee.

Order of the British Empire. Not surprisingly, she was also on the Fife committee of the Queen Alexandra Memorial Nursing Fund. After her husband's death she spent a lot of time in her native Australia, but it was in Kilmany that she died in 1958 at the age of eighty-six. She was remembered by the villagers for the natural, unaffected way in which she talked to them.

Robert Bruce worked on the estate for many years and in retirement in the Dairy House told of the Colonel's fear of his house catching fire. He had a large ornamental lake dug in his grounds, one reason being to provide a ready supply of water. He also obtained fire fighting equipment such as pumps and hoses. After some years there was a fire and workers duly rushed to man the pumps and hoses. Unfortunately through disuse the hoses had rotted, so that the real Fire Brigade had to be summoned after all. Bruce's daughter, Martha, tells of the Saturday evenings between the wars when Jimmy Shand would come out from Auchtermuchty with his band, sit on the roadside bank outside Wester Kilmany Farmhouse and play while the locals danced on the highway as a ballroom. Sometimes there were Socials in the Squash Court beside the Dairy Cottage. In those days before the Tay Road Bridge opened in 1966 there was very little traffic on the main road. Indeed Eric Young recalls boys playing football on it, and declaring half time if a car came along.[131]

Colonel Anstruther-Gray died in April 1938 after a short illness having attended a Council meeting in Cupar only three weeks earlier. The local press regarded him as "a kind and courteous gentleman in every sense of the word" who "formed and retained a vast circle of friends in all walks of life." Perhaps Kilmany had never seen anything like the funeral which was taken by the Rector of the Episcopalian church in Newport, with burial in a personal addition to Kilmany churchyard. Special arrangements had to be made to park all the cars, and the coffin was brought from the house on a farm wagon draped in evergreen branches. A strong turn out of the county was led by the Earl of Lindsay, together with farmers, villagers and estate workers. The coffin was carried by eight of these: James Denholm, J. Henderson and J. Melville, gardeners; J. Stalker and W. Stalker, gamekeepers; Stewart Bernard and Robert Bruce,

---

131 Personal communications between 1968 and 2009.

foresters, and R. Payne, chauffeur. Thirty years later, it was all still so vivid in his memory when Robert Bruce recalled that the coffin was so heavy that he had helped to carry it on a board before it was lowered in to the grave by the aristocratic pall-bearers led by the only son and heir.

The new laird, also William, had been member of Parliament for Lanarkshire since 1931. He spent a great deal of time in London during a Parliamentary career in both Houses which would stretch ahead for more than half a century, but Kilmany remained his home and the centre of his family. This long period was interrupted by his return to active service and he was awarded the Military Cross. Losing his seat at the landslide Labour victory of 1945, he was returned to Parliament again, for a different constituency, Berwick and East Lothian, in 1950. He was of the backbone of the Conservative party. Though he never held high office he became Chairman of the 1922 Committee, and through his wife, Monica Lambton, was closely related to Lord Home, the Conservative Prime Minister from 1963–64.

While Member for Berwick and East Lothian Anstruther-Gray was opposed at one election by the Labour candidate, John Mackintosh, who recalled that he was approached in Haddington by his Tory opponent, a quintessential knight of the shires. "They tell me you're going about the constituency making speeches about politics, Mackintosh," he said in kindly tones. "It won't do, you know."[132] Mackintosh, the academic political scientist, told the story wryly against himself. "I think the old boy may have been right," he used to say. Mackintosh was not elected. Created a baronet in 1958, Sir William Anstruther-Grays's closing years in the Commons were spent as Deputy Speaker, and he was created a Life Peer as Lord Kilmany in 1966.

He had a great interest in horse racing and was elected to the National Hunt Committee in 1948. At one time he kept seventeen horses, the best known of them being Mischievous Monk and his last official appointment was as Lord Lieutenant of Fife from 1975 until 1980. Always active in the Lords, he was taken ill there one June day in 1985, having set out from Kilmany that morning. He

---

[132] Quoted by Ian McIntyre in 'Govan's seismic shock', in *The Times*, 12 November 1988.

died in London a few days later. Lady Kilmany had received the O.B.E. for her War work. Locally she was much involved in politics as a County Councillor, and with horses. She had had a serious riding accident some months before and did not long outlive him. They had two daughters. The Honourable Mrs Weir, who inherited the big house and in 1986 divided it into two parts known as Kilmany House and West Kilmany House, and the Honourable Mrs McNab of McNab.

The World Champion Racing Driver, Jim Clark, was usually represented as being of Border farming stock, but no account of this period would be complete without dwelling on the most famous man to be born in Kilmany during the Twentieth Century. In fact his father had become tenant farmer to the Anstruther-Grays at Wester Kilmany in 1931, and Jim was born in that house five years later. He grew up in a deep-rooted Presbyterian culture for his father was a kirk elder and also the Session Clerk at Kilmany throughout his eleven years here. Young Jim went to the village school, and the Border connection only began when his father bought a farm near Duns in 1942, moving the family there.[133] In his last six years of racing with the Lotus Team he was third twice, second once, and World Champion in 1963 and 1965. Colin Chapman, the founder of Lotus cars described him as "the finest man I ever knew. As a driver he was a complete genius. And you, know, I doubt if he ever fully realised it."[134]

A hundred years before Clark's birth, the minister had written that "from an early period, Kilmany has been an agricultural parish, and its population possessed of much natural talent,

40 JIM CLARK, by David Annand in the village.

---

133 Dymock, E. *Jim Clark: Tribute a to Champion*, Sutton Verney (1997) pp. 49–53.

134 Quoted in Nye, D. *Jim Clark*, Richmond (1991) p. 168.

great industry, and pious and amiable dispositions."[135] Though brought up in such a home, the racing champion was not confirmed into the Church of Scotland until after he had left school, and his parish minister bore witness to the sincerity of his on-going Christian faith and commitment. The memorial plaque in Loretto School Chapel was dedicated with words which all ring true,

> To the glory of God and in memory of
> Jim Clark,
> former pupil of the school
> World Champion racing driver,
> true friend, trusted team-mate,
> Christian gentleman,
> a man after God's own heart.[136]

Though the *Old* (1795) and *New* (1845) *Statistical Accounts* spanned half a century, they essentially reflected the same rural world. After a long interval, the *Third Statistical Account* was published in 1952, although the information had been gathered by 1947.[137] It therefore reflects the situation immediately after the end of the Second World War. The scene portrayed is markedly different from that of its predecessors but, reading it now after another fifty odd years have passed, we see that much has changed out of all recognition. After that war the age old system of ownership remained. From the inhabitants of the Manse downwards the people lived in tied houses. Most of these dwellings had been modernised (this seems to have meant piped water from the nearby spring replacing wells, and toilet facilities instead of outside dry closets) and were occupied by active workers on the land. It was rare to find old and retired people. Though the main high tension cable passed through Kilmany, apart from farms few could afford the electricity supply. The Manse was still lit by paraffin lamps, and the village was not supplied until 1958.

Children over 12 tears of age were bussed to Bell Baxter in Cupar, though for many years none had gone on to university. There were still plenty of children to maintain the two primary schools. All the teachers were women, since the last schoolmaster left in 1942.

---

135 Cook, H. D. *op. cit.* p. 544.

136 Gauld, G., *Jim Clark – The Legend Lives On*, Northamptonshire, 3rd Ed. (1989) Appendix One pp. 135–138.

137 Smith, A. *The Third Statistical Account of Scotland,* Edinburgh (1952).

Kilmany had one teacher and 18 pupils while at Rathillet there were two teachers with 32 children, though numbers fluctuated because of the fluid population of farm workers. It was noted that at a Centenary Service for the death of Chalmers in 1947, only the family of the Session Clerk was descended from those of his time.

The Re-unification of the Church of Scotland in 1929 meant that the churches at Kilmany and Rathillet were under the one minister from 1934. By the end of the Second World War the services were poorly attended, apart from communions. There were Sunday schools in both churches, but no Bible Class, and the Youth Club had recently ceased. The minister at this time was the Revd Ian Henderson, who would be the third to go on to a university Professorship, this time at Glasgow. During his years at Kilmany he was inspired by Chalmers' profound interest in the social problems of his day. This led Henderson on to research that period himself, particularly the conditions created by the industrial revolution. However, he held rather different theological views from Chalmers. As a young man he had come under the influence of the Swiss theologian Karl Barth, and became his translator here.

Young people who did not want to work on the land had to travel to Cupar or Dundee for employment. There were ten such in 1947. Despite much better public transport than nowadays, eight of these could only get to work on time by cycling. The North Fife Railway provided two trains daily to Perth and Dundee plus an extra afternoon train to Dundee on Saturdays. There was a bus through Kilmany from Cupar to Newport three times a day, with extra services on Tuesday, Saturday, and Sunday. On those days there was also a Newburgh to Cupar service.

In Kilmany there was the post Office, and there was still a Wilson as blacksmith, who was glad to have an assistant when he could get one. There was no shop, though vans came out from Cupar shops, as they did for many years. Today there is only the fishmonger on Fridays from Pittenweem.

The parish was still entirely agricultural and the 55 two-horse ploughs of Old Statistical Account a hundred and fifty years earlier had not been entirely replaced, for there were still 50 horses along with 32 tractors. The land was now divided into 18 holdings, compared with the 14 in Chalmers' time, and nine were farmed by the owners. A distinctive characteristic of the landscape in 1947 was

41 KILMANY STATION 1968, disused with track removed (since built over with three houses). The Stationmaster's House remains.

42 THE REVEREND JACK AND MRS NANCY SCROGGIE with Mrs Stewart of The Gauldry (Organist) in 1968. He was the last minister to live in the manse and after he moved to Dundee in 1969 it was sold.

43 THE MUSEUM AND LAUNDRY, formerly the shoemaker's house and workshop, derelict and crumbling in July 1968, and likely to disappear.

44 COTTAGES AND BOTHY derelict in 1968. The remnants of a second bothy stand in the foreground. Compare these photographs with illustration 19 on page 54.

due to the fact that during the war the woods on the **Kilmany** and **Myrecarnie** hills had been felled, and recently those behind **Mountquhanie** House and on **Murdocairnie** Hill. As there had yet been no fresh planting the aspect would have appeared to us unusually bare.

The most active voluntary meetings in the area were for women. The Church had a branch of the Women's Guild, while a flourishing branch of the Women's Rural Institute had a membership of fifty. Meetings alternating at Kilmany and Rathillet averaged around thirty. In comparison the Men's Club, which had weekly meetings at Kilmany in the winter, and a Burn's Supper, was in decline. An entertainment by local talent on Old Year's Night, with admission only by ticket, was still described as an outstanding success as many liked to return from elsewhere to come to it. Into the 1970s Guy Fawkes' Night was still publicly celebrated with a large bonfire built in preceding days by estate workers.

The Account concluded: "Kilmany today may be summed up as a prosperous agricultural community, healthy to live in, with a population whose friendliness and good sense are noteworthy, and who are better off than many similar areas for the amenities of life."

Like many rural villages Kilmany has suffered further depopulation. By the 1960s at least one old cottage had recently been demolished; that on the opposite corner of The Wynd was derelict, having last been used as kennels. Little more could be said for what is now known as Loaning Hill. Mrs Grieve, the first and last laundry woman left in 1958, and it stood empty for ten years, becoming increasingly derelict and overgrown. According to David Christie, Lord Kilmany's grieve at Easter Kilmany, it too would have been removed had it not be bought, the first house in the village to be sold, and the first step in halting the decline. The sawmill had moved to Cupar about the beginning of the First World War (possibly as part of the development of Kilmany House with the desire to end the noise of the sawmill), and the last joiner died before the Second. In 1962 Dr Beeching closed the railway, and March of 1969 saw the last minister, Jack Scroggie, leave the Manse. It was sold in 1971 to the solicitor, John Scott of Dundee, and has since been known as Kilmany Grange. Having long been tenants, the Whitefords bought Wester Kilmany in 1989.

The Post Office closed in 1981 with Mrs Brown's retirement.

She was then over ninety and her time with the Post Office, though not continuous, had spanned seventy years. To those of us who remember her in those final years she seemed to be the last of the old time Kilmany villagers, and nobly she represented them, with such a bright, loveable and contented personality. The warmth of her welcome to newcomers was very moving, and she was notorious for watching television far into the night. But she had been born into another age, having come into the world in March 1889 in the house which still stands next to the church and opposite the smithy. Within a month she had been baptised there in the Christian names Margaret Mitchell, her mother's maiden name. She had brothers two years older and two years younger than herself, and her mother was twice pregnant within a month of her near neighbour, Christine Wilson, wife of the blacksmith. Her father, Nathan Duncan, was the village joiner. He later lost an arm in an accident at the nearby sawmill and went on to succeed Alexander Rogers in keeping the Post Office, two doors away from the smithy. He was also the parish Registrar. At the age of twenty-one she was married in Kilmany church to David Rolland Brown, a railway signalman from St Andrews. The proclamation of their marriage was on Christmas Day 1910 and they were married five days later. Her husband died suddenly in the signal box at St Fort in 1945 and Mrs Brown spent the long years of her widowhood continuing to run the Post Office and selling home-made fudge for the fun of it. Now she lies in the old churchyard, a few yards from where she was born. Her grave is unmarked, but her memory survives as the last of the life-long Kilmany villagers who can stand in celebration of them all. Soon after her retirement the

45 MRS BROWN of the Post Office and Mrs Grieve (with handbag) who died in 1968.

School was closed and sold off. With further reorganisation of the parishes worship in the church was reduced to alternate Sundays. Of the four principle features mentioned by McGonagall, only the Church remains.

Against this trend we have seen the building of Motray Lodge, the restoration of the sawmill house (which was later a dairy), the old Post Office and the School, and David Annand rebuilding on The Wynd, new life in Kilmany House and more children in the village. Most recently restored has been the Gardener's Cottage, and more still needs to be done. The old feudal set-up which was still evident in Kilmany village even thirty years ago, has disappeared. Instead of the Justice of the Peace in the big house, he is now to be found among those with noteworthy artistic talent.

Chalmers had grown very fond of the area where he first ministered and its beauty, expressing the view of many in stating that it was somewhere where he would be glad to grow old in.[138] We

46 THE ANSTRUTHER-GRAYS' SQUASH COURT beside the Dairy between the Wars. This was later used as a small village hall for social events, and the gable end was surmounted by a large weather vane in the shape of a huntsman with dogs. After severe damage by the falling of a tree the vane was removed and the building decayed. It has since been restored as part of the Dairy Cottage complex, but lacks both vane and porch. Beyond the Cottage is the Public Baths demolished *circa* 1960.

---

138 Hanna, *op. cit.* Vol.1, p. 445.

are reminded in our family of its continuing beauty. In a six week period in July and August 1979, Jean and Catriona named over a hundred wild flowers growing in the vicinity.

Further mention can be made of the railway. This latter day branch line ran from the junction at St Fort to Newburgh, thus making a link between Dundee and Perth south of the Tay and also enabling trains to run from Perth to St Andrews. Though in fact it only ever dealt in "potatoes and the excursion traffic", it was built in expectation that the villages it linked, Kilmany, Luthrie, and Lindores would develop as dormitory settlements for those commuting to Dundee and Perth. That never happened, and the line was never profitable. Its construction was a very considerable undertaking, and included the two signal boxes and three sets of signals around St Fort station on the extreme eastern border of the parish. Known as the Newburgh and North Fife Railway, its trains were actually run by the North British. Opened in 1909, regular passenger traffic ceased in 1951. In its last decade the track occasionally carried special excursion trains, and the station was converted into holiday letting. A girl who came there with her family remembered that drivers of passing goods trains would stop and call out, "Do you want any coal?" and, if so, obligingly left some. As late as the early 1980s, young Robin and I could still set off along the line of the old track and walk right through to Lindores only having to descend from the embankment wherever a former bridge across a road had been dismantled. By now much of the embankment has been breeched for the convenience of farmers or disappeared altogether.

Finally, with the younger Cook, we celebrate the location:
> The climate of Kilmany, from its situation, is mild and pleasant. The heat in summer, in the morning, and forenoon, is sometimes oppressive; but not often so; by the afternoon, the wind goes round to the east, and gives us a cooling breeze from the German Ocean. The cold in winter is seldom intense. ...[139]

---

139 Cook, H. D. *op. cit.* p. 534.

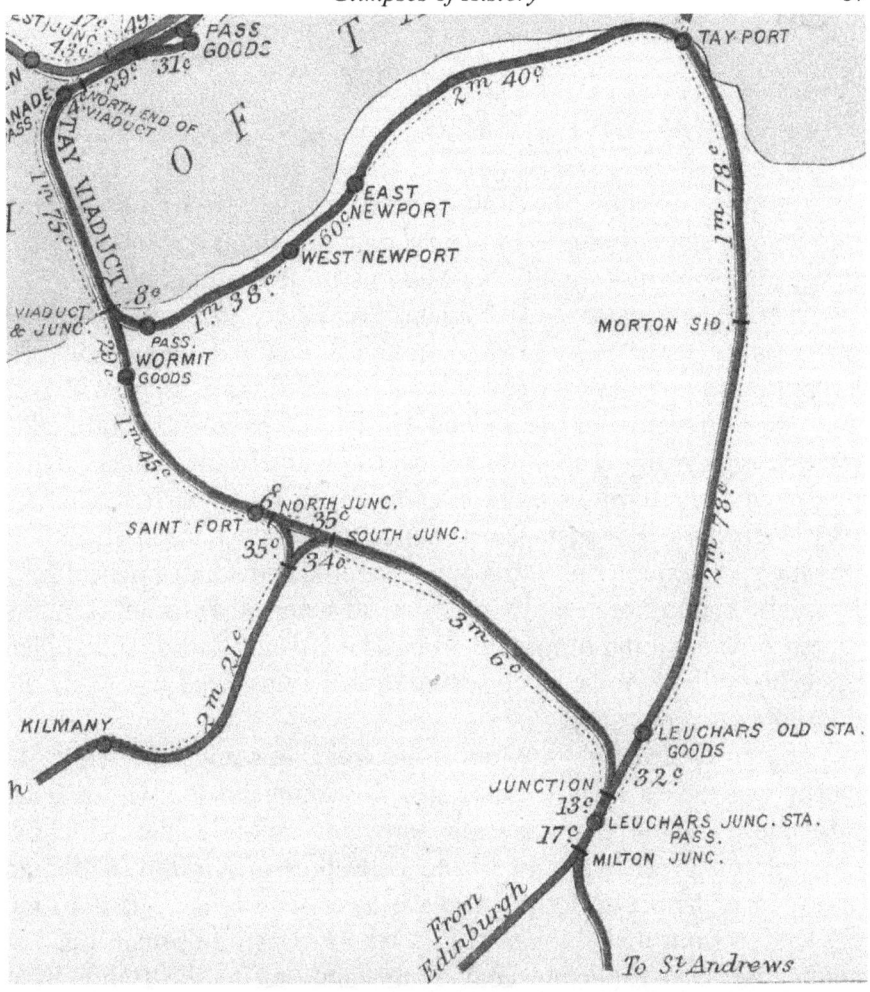

47 THE NEWBURGH AND NORTH FIFE RAILWAY branching off from the London to Aberdeen line (North British) at St Fort for Kilmany, going on (not shown) to Luthrie, and Lindores before linking up with Newburgh and on to Perth and Inverness. There was a small goods yard at Rathillet.

EPILOGUE: ADVENTURERS, VILLAINS, AND HEROES

A little more is added here about some of the key figures already mentioned, and in order to include something about one or two other individuals who also qualify beneath this triple heading.

The social history of Kilmany reflected in most of these glimpses is far removed from anything that we know now. Its structure did not really begin to break up until the First World War and lingered even after the Second. Life in the parish was dominated by a few men of wealth, joined occasionally by an heiress. Only they, and their families were ever likely to travel far from where they were born. For instance, Helenus and Lady Gibson (page 18) travelled to London and Paris for leisure, and to Bath for health.[140] In such a rural area only the minister and the tenant farmers represented any kind of middle class. The artisans, those with skilled trades were likely to be more secure than the unskilled who were the poor, the great majority.

The class structure was not quite rigid, but few rose within it, and it was easier to fall, especially for younger sons who had no inheritance. Some families came upwardly mobile into Kilmany. One interesting case is that of the Gillespies of Kirkton in Forgan and then of **Mountquhanie** who we have seen (page 39) not long descended from that skipper in Elie who prospered through making annual voyages exporting coal, grain, and salt to the Baltic from where he imported iron, and timber, and to Bordeaux whence he brought wine. He left a Journal of these activities. In 1677 he acquired the estate of Newton Rires and built a notable house in Elie where James, Duke of York (afterwards James II) is said to have stayed.[141] In the eighteenth and nineteenth centuries the Gillespies

---

140 Halkerston, H. *An Appeal to Reason*, Edinburgh (1778) p. 13.

141 University of St Andrews has a web-site on Gillespie and the researches of Dr Paula Martin. By a curious co-incidence it seems that the estate of Wester Newton Rires which passed to others when the Gillespies moved to Kirkton of Forgan, was in 1713 acquired by John Thomson, the first of Newton, later being renamed Charleton, the principal seat of the Anstruther Thomson family much referred to above, see Millar, *op.cit.* II. p.21.

were the largest land owners in the parish of Kilmany. A lesser example is to be found in the Lauries who became tenants at **Hillcairnie** in 1720 and over a long stay acquired the lairdship.

In between those two estates is **Rathillet** where the Halkerstons were on the way down. Of course, when the then head of the family, David Halkerston or Hackston (page 13), was condemned in 1680 the estate was forfeited. However, next in line was his brother William, episcopal minister at Cleish in Kinross, of opposite views to Convenanters like David, and loyal to the Stuarts. Moreover the family were cousins germaine to the Earl of Rothes, among the most powerful in Scotland, who was made a Duke shortly before David's death. Through such influence William was soon restored to Rathillet, but two generations on we have already taken note of the eccentricities of his grandson, Helenus. Ignoring the claims of his only child who never married, and the close collateral men in the family, he gave Rathillet away in return for a very uncertain life rent for himself.[142] No longer lairds, we shall soon see one of them as a tenant of the Gillespies. In a later generation, another was fortunate enough to marry the head of the Carswells, the family who had obtained Rathillet soon after Helenus had lost it, but that was only a temporary return.

However, it was from among all the classes that a few adventurous spirits set out from Kilmany for destinations elsewhere, sometimes even beyond Fife, not knowing whither their steps would take them, and how they would fare for themselves or their offspring. There must have been others whose stories have not come down to us, or have not yet come to light, but a few are known.

There was the minister, John Sharp (page 11) journeying from Kilmany to Aberdeen in defiance of his King for conscience sake. This led him on to imprisonment in Blackness Castle followed by many years of exile abroad, and finally to a Chair at the University of Edinburgh.

The minsters sent a steady stream of offspring to foreign places. William Smibert, also laird of **Lochmalony**, had two sons, John and William who succeeded him there in turn. Possibly both were army officers, and William certainly was. He served in America during the years before the Revolution only to return home to die childless

---

142 Halkerston, *op. cit.* (1777).

in Cupar in 1776.[143] Lairds often kept town houses, either there or, if wealthier, in Edinburgh. Thus in 1814 David Gillespie (page 40) was born there[144] and not at Mountquhanie, though his father was not an absentee laird.

Smibert's successor, M'Cormick (1760) was of short duration here but would have a daughter married in Madras in 1805. Adamson (1764–1772), had a son, born in Kilmany who died in Calcutta, and another who died in the East Indies. John Cook (1793–1802) had a son commissioned in the Madras Infantry who died there in 1838. All of these will have set out full of hope from St Andrews since their fathers had moved there by the time of their departure. Cook's brother, Henry David (1815–1857) had a son born here in 1840 who died in Adelaide in 1918.[145]

Tenant farmers were another source of adventurers further afield. James Balfour came from the eldest branch of a Leuchars family of farmers, but spent many years as a tenant in Kilmany, and was an Elder who supported Adamson during the rebuilding of the Church in 1768. He had a son Alexander, born here but breaking away from a farming background, who prospered mightily as a Dundee merchant, became Chief Magistrate (Provost) 1826–1828, and a Deputy Lieutenant for the county. Within a couple more generations, these Balfours were possessed of the estate of Dawyck (now with its famous Garden) in the Borders near Peebles. The upward mobility of this family is further demonstrated in that the Barons Kinross descend from James's uncle, and the Balfour Baronets from his younger brother.

Others crossed the sea. We have seen a young Edie dying in India and another emigrating to Canada. It is no great surprise that Captain Hugh Pearson, R.N., who was possessed of **Myrecairnie** (page 25), died at Vellore in 1838, but more so that his fourth daughter should have died there two years before at the age of ten.[146]

---

143 *Fasti* for Sharp and Smibert. It has John in the 26th Regiment of Foot, but no profession for William. No such record for John has been found, but *Army Lists* for this period are scant. William is listed with the Regiment in *Army Lists* at The National Archives, Kew; William's will, Register House, Edinburgh.

144 Census returns give place of birth.

145 Details of the children are in *Fasti*.

146 *The Fifeshire Journal*; 8 September 1836 & January 1839.

It would be interesting to know why Pearson was spending time there with his family. After his death some of his sons made for Australia and settled in Gippsland. Hugh had previously followed his father into the Royal Navy, but died there in 1856. William was born in Kilmany in 1818. At twenty-two he sailed from Greenock to Adelaide, a voyage which lasted for nine months. Settling in Gippsland, over the next half century he prospered and was for many years a member of the Legislative Assembly. He features in the *Australian Dictionary of Biography*.[147]

Another of the heritor families were the Horsburghs of Lochmalony. When the bachelor laird, James died in 1868 he was succeeded by his brother Dr Boyd Horsburgh who had no interest in the property and soon sold it. Altogether there had been eight brothers in this Kilmany family, and two at least of them had gone out to live in Goulburn, New South Wales where Boyd died in 1887 and Henry 1894.

Reasons for going varied but always there was the hope of betterment. Young John Dewar, born here among the labourers in 1813 and training as a shoemaker, was drawn into enlisting in the Cameron Highlanders when they came recruiting into Cupar which is Black Watch country. Surely he was not the first Kilmany man to go for a soldier. John's enlistment led him far away, firstly, of course, to Sutherland where he married a girl from Tongue and to some fifteen years with the Colours, in eight of which he was stationed in "North America" that is in Canada. During his length of service he won two good conduct badges with extra pay and was promoted to Corporal. Two years before his regiment acquired fame in the Crimea, he was invalided as Chelsea Pensioner for reasons of sickness considered wholly honourable and including "a strenuous habit of body."[148] Having lost a leg, he returned to live out a long life in Kilmany as Beadle at the Church, and with the unusual advantage of a secure pension. For many years his wife was the only English and Gaelic speaker in the parish.

The Kirks were for long the blacksmiths at Hazelton Walls. Eventually the work passed to two brothers, Thomas and William,

---

147 'Fife Deaths Abroad 1850–1917', typescript in Cupar Reference Library (hereafter CRL).

148 Record in The National Archives, Kew; Census Returns; Kilmany Kirk Session Minutes.

but by the middle of the nineteenth century, both having raised families, it was difficult to support them all. In the 1860s, and already in his fifties, William Kirk took the bold step of emigrating to Australia while his wife was again pregnant, his last child being born on the voyage which seems not to have been an easy one. Having arrived safely, the captain became the subject of a formal complaint. Many passengers supported this, while others equally wrote in his defence.[149]

After another score of years there was perhaps an even bolder venture. Robert Aitken was securely well-established as tenant farmer at Easter Kilmany and had fairly recently embarked on another nineteen year lease. He startled Kilmany with news of his intended departure, leaving his sister to honour his agreement, a rather unusual arrangement at the time, and emigrated to Colorado. The days of the fabled Gold Rush were over but veins around Ouvray were still rich in gold, silver, zinc and other metals. Moreover his timing was good for the heyday there for mining lasted from 1881 to 1893. Aitken was based at the El Mahdi Mine and died there in 1891 ten years after his arrival.[150] It is not known how far his venture succeeded, but sister Isabella carried on the farming for fourteen more years, only retiring to Newport in 1895 two years short of term.[151]

Perhaps he began to think of a radical move after the example of another of the Kilmany tenants. The father and grandfather of George Anderson had leased **Mountquhanie** for nearly seventy years and he served the same lairds at **Drumnod**, following the versatile John Haxton there, both farmer and journalist.[152] George abandoned the parish of his fathers first for Canada in 1872, and then for Kansas living out his life for over thirty years still farming. George Watt stayed put at Wester Kilmany, but his eldest son, John, left Kilmany in the same year as Aitken for a life in South Africa. Five years later in far off Natal he married his sweetheart from

---

149 Personal communication from the Kirk family in Australia, since destroyed; Census Returns 1861 show them still here.

150 *The Fifeshire Journal*, 6 May 1891.

151 Details about the Aitkens in a bundle of 37 tacks, agreements, etc. of J. A. Thomson of Charleton, 1826–1909: University of St Andrews Archive MS38395. The reserved right for a new road (page 70) is in the same.

152 *The Fifeshire Journal*, 27 March 1856, p. 5.

Springfield, near Cupar. That must have been some romance and they lived together for half a century.

Ebenezer, a younger son of Carswell of Rathillet, laird, hands on farmer and J.P, died in middle life on the far off North West frontier of India in 1894. John Page, the eldest son of a tenant at **Myrecairnie** died in New Zealand in 1870. Betsy Wilson, daughter of the Kilmany blacksmith married into the same trade in Largo, but the young couple were drawn to Australia and settled in Victoria where she died in 1884. Isabella, daughter of the old Kilmany family of Kilgour, married a gardener and they emigrated to Massachusetts where she died at Salem in 1881.

A little earlier than these last named was James Thomson Robertson who left his native Kilmany in 1847 for Australia. He finally settled in Gippsland. Did he know the Pearsons who were already there? Having secured land, he made his home there. A prospector and pastoralist, he and his eldest son were pioneer explorers of the Snowy River which is now a National Park.[153]

Such, and no doubt some others, were the few; but for most Gray's words apply":

Far from the madding crowd's ignoble strife,
Their sober wishes never learned to stray;
Along the cool sequestered vale of life
They kept the noiseless tenor of their way.

This they did in and around Kilmany, or no further afield than by crossing the waters of the Tay lured on by prospects real or illusory which might await them there in Dundee.

So much for some of the adventurers, but what can be said of the villains?

Most of us enjoy a good fictional murder story, but the Parish of Kilmany has been well endowed with reprobates on the public stage. We have seen Alexander Lindsay implicated in the death of Lord Lindsay, the heir to a powerful earldom, the Balfours of Moutquhanie involved in the murder of Cardinal Beaton, and Haxton of Rathlllet in that of Archbishop Sharp. Stories of spectres in Ghoules' Den may be rather fanciful, but there is nothing unreal about the haunting recollection of these past brutalities perpetrated or condoned by men of the parish.

Here we need to return to these Balfours and two of the sons of

---

153 For all these see CRL.

that Andrew who was laird of Mountquhanie for seventy-nine years in the sixteenth century. While very young he inherited from his grandfather killed at Flodden, and lived to a great age. His eldest son was Sir Michael who died before him, but he had other sons. The most notorious, and villainous was James,[154] known to history as Sir James Balfour of Pittendreich. Presumably born and brought up at the castle here, at an early age he joined his father, and some of his brothers at St Andrews Castle in May 1546, after the murder of Cardinal Beaton, holding it for the cause of reform. When it fell, he was among those imprisoned and sent to work in the French galleys. Another brother there, and notorious intriguer, became Sir Gilbert Balfour of Westray, greatly enriched by Church lands in the Orkneys given after the Reformation, and sometime Master of the Queen's household.

Once freed, James Balfour then espoused the Catholic cause and being in priest's orders began a career in ecclesiastical law. To this he soon added the revenues from the Vicarage of Kilmany to which he was appointed in 1555.[155] Thus he was the last of the incumbents under Rome, though we cannot know whether he ever conducted any of the services and other parochial duties most likely left to a paid assistant. Nevertheless he was in name, and in fact, the last Vicar of Kilmany. With the Reformation, from 1560 the duties were taken on by a Protestant Minister, but the revenues of the Vicarage remained with Balfour. He now claimed to be a Lutheran. Rising to high office and knighted, amongst other things he was a secretary to Mary, Queen of Scots who believed that it had been intended that he should be killed along with Rizzio in 1566. Then James, supporting Bothwell against "King Henry" Darnley, the husband of Mary, became deeply involved in his death in 1567.

Aspects of the murder remain a mystery, but James and his younger brother, Robert, were both involved and Gilbert, too, it is

---

154 P. G. B. McNeil in his *ODNB* article erroneously has him as the son of his brother Sir Michael. *Registrum Secreti Sigilli Regum Scotorum (Registers of the Privy Seal of Scotland]) (RSSRS)* 1567–1574 Vol. VI edited by Donaldson, G., Edinburgh 1963, p. 249 clearly has Robert as son of Andrew, and ibid, 1575–80 Vol. VII edited by Donaldson, G., Edinburgh (1966), p. 349 has him brother of James of Pittendreich.

155 Haws, C.H., *Scottish Parish Clergy at the Reformation 1540–1574*, Edinburgh (1972), p. 128.

said. Having been estranged, Darnley came to visit Mary in Edinburgh but was suffering from smallpox and could not stay at Holyrood. Only weeks before, Robert had become Provost of St Mary's, Kirk o' Field nearby, giving him possession of the buildings.[156] Darnley was lodged there. On the night of 10 February 1567 he was disturbed, and escaping into the garden, was murdered. A loud explosion followed but Darnley was already dead.

All this remains an intriguing and unsolved mystery. Many have thought then and since that James was a key figure in the plot. In 1571 both James and Robert were forfeited and "put to the horn" (banished). The shadowy Robert seems to have suffered simply through being the owner of the property where Darnley died and the brother of a rogue. A few years previously, James had passed the revenues from the Vicarage of Kilmany to Robert who now lost them, of course, in the attainder. Through double-dealing James was soon restored, and curiously again received the Kilmany revenues presumably at his brother's expense.

Suspicion dogged James for the rest of his life which is a catalogue of intrigue, betrayals, forfeiture and restoration, during which he continued with notable legal work.[157] In 1579 the forfeiture was renewed but again rescinded after a couple of years, so that he was still in possession of the Kilmany revenues when he died in 1583. Latterly he claimed to be a Presbyterian. A man of many mysteries and other killings he was instrumental in such fatal matters as the Craigmillar bond, the Casket Letters, and the downfall and execution of the Regent Morton. His career has been described as "one of the blackest in the annals of political perfidy and crime" but he died in his bed "a repeated religious and political turncoat," and not a son of whom Kilmany can be proud.

In contrast, one of the obvious heroes in the previous pages is Robert Lumsden of Mountquhanie (see pages 38-39), ruling Elder of the Church of Kilmany, and in command of Dundee for the King in

---

156 For his appointment, see *RSSRS*, Vol. XXXV 1566 fol.95; the *Fasti* has him wrongly described as Provost of St Mary's, the College in the University at St Andrews.

157 Details of Pittendreich's life are well known. The article in the *ODNB* serves, and there are books like MacRobert, A. F., *Mary Queen of Scots* and the Casket Letters, London, (2002) and Bingham, C., *Darnley*, London (1995) where Darnley's murder and the involvement of the Balfours is discussed.

1651. After a military career in Swedish service, he took up arms for Charles II and was captured at Dunbar, being ill-treated as a prisoner before his release. Forced to surrender a second time while a combatant after his heroic last stand in the Old Tower of the Church of Dundee, he could probably not have expected to be spared despite the assurances it is said he was given. Ironically he was opposed by Monck, who had once been a King's officer and a decade later received a dukedom having changed sides once more. Lumsden wrote a letter while incarcerated in Dundee which is a model of patriotic appeal to Monck to return to his first allegiance.[158]

The other heroes no doubt include Thomas Chalmers who inspired many in his generation and since, Alexander Paterson who contracted mortal illness through compassion in aiding the poor, and Jim Clark the winner of many a race who tragically died in a practice run,[159] and there are the two World Wars.[160]

Among the women there were no doubt many unsung heroines

---

158 See also pp. 8 & 38; Kilmany Kirk Session Minutes; Millar, *op. cit.* II, p. 313 for the letter.

159 For these men, see entries in the Index.

160 The Kilmany War Memorial at Rathillet bears eight names from the First conflict. The Donaldson brothers grew up in farm cottages at Easter Kinnear and died with the Scots Guards. In the Second war, Graham Henderson, eldest son of the land-owning farmer there was commissioned from school into The Royal Engineers and volunteered to serve with a unit using top-secret weapons. Killed in action in 1944, his name was placed on the Roll of Honour in Kilmany Church, but it is troubling that nothing was added to the stone cross at Rathillet. Seventy years later his younger brother, Michael, has discovered that in his first action, the battle for Le Havre, Graham received several wounds from a mortar, but did not seek treatment until next day "because he was too busy." Moving rapidly into Holland, he joked about having lost three more 'lives' before his unit was involved in the battle for Venray. With his Captain recently disabled, he was in command. On the morning of the 16 October his troop was assigned to bridge a small river, and reconnoitring the foundations he was hit by a sniper. Having been bandaged by an infantry officer he was killed by a mortar bomb when returning to his tank. Through his inspiration, his troop successfully laid the bridge, allowing the advance to continue. His senior officer wrote, "always calm" he "never seemed to know the meaning of the word danger" and "would certainly have got a Military Cross had he lived." He was only twenty years of age. Now this gallant young man's name will be added at Rathillet, as it should have been long ago, through the help of Councillor Tim Brett, the Session Clerk at the Church. (Michael Henderson of Easter Kinnear provided details of Graham.)

whose stories have not come down to us, but one has been written about. In the 1750s a widow with three young children came to Kilmany from the Highlands. Despite this being so soon after the last Jacobite upheaval, a kindly farmer gave her a free cottage, and her children grew up and began to fend for themselves. One was Annie, a cowherd and serving girl, who was greatly influenced by successive ministers, William Smibert and then John Adamson. At twenty-five she married James Christie, a farm worker from the parish. Like many such employees, he moved around at the hirings, and the family settled in Monimail. Though soon widowed, Annie lived on there to an advanced age greatly beloved for her kindliness and acts of Christian charity. So great was her influence for good that her last minister there, James Brodie, wrote up and published *A Memoir of Annie M'Donald Christie – a self taught cottager*.[161] There will have been others such of whom we now know nothing, but her story can stand for the rest.

NOTE ON HOUSE NAMES IN KILMANY

With apologies to present owners, house names were virtually unknown historically in such a rural setting. Almost all buildings were owned by the estate of which they were a part. Except for those with long term occupational names like the Post Office, Smithy, and Dairy, here in the hamlet of Kilmany cottages were simply known by the present occupier. Anyone who has looked at old Census returns will know how difficult it can be to identify the exact location in which named individuals were living because of the lack of either house name or number. Similarly the lanes had no street name. The signs for 'The Wynd' were no doubt erected when four Council houses were compulsorily built at Wynd's End, and numbered. As for the old cottages, all such names as Keeper's, Gardener's, Stables, for us Loaning Hill (and there are others), are modern inventions. Keeper's is merely where the last gamekeeper, very aptly called Mr Stalker, died sadly disabled and in retirement about 1969. The real keeper's cottage had been in the heart of Ghoules' Den. In 1968 Gardener's (not known as such) was occupied by "Old Margaret" the housekeeper. What is now the derelict Stables Cottage, was the real Gardener's house for Kilmany Cottage (precursor of the present House). Occupied within living

---

161 Edinburgh (1849).

memory, it was turned into a stables half a century ago for more of Lord Kilmany's horses. Pigscrave is a modern replacement for a previously unnamed cottage (last used as kennels), adjacent to the site of one of a considerable number of such porcine shelters. Manses were sold with a requirement that they should not become the Old Manse. In Kilmany it became the Grange, while that at Rathillet became Grayson, contracting personal names. Even to the end of their lives Lord and Lady Kilmany headed their letters 'Kilmany'. The terms 'Kilmany House' and 'West Kilmany House' have come into use more recently. 'Loaning Hill' was cobbled together in great haste. In 1968 we told friends that we had bought a cottage in Kilmany. Innocently, they wrote to us at 'The Cottage, Kilmany.' Though it was fifty years since the historic Kilmany Cottage (of which we had then never heard) had been transformed into 'the Big House', confusion over the delivery of post still occurred apparently because of us, hence the rapid need for a distinctive name at his Lordship's request. Motray Cottage was suggested by the Grieve, but we were too far from that stream. The Old Laundry only celebrated a fairly ephemeral use for part of this old building; indeed after it was established, and as long as he lived, the accommodation was known as the 'under-gardener's' after the husband's occupation. Before the 1920s it had had quite other uses in its long history.[162] So for better or worse something reflecting the location was hurriedly put together and, before we knew it, this had become enshrined on large scale Ordnance Survey maps! Equally unknown to us, and more surprisingly perhaps, was the conspiracy by BT and GPO, once the Internet had begun to operate. They transformed the name into Loaning Hill House, and as it is enshrined there for ever, from this there can now be no return.

---

162 About the time of the death of the last shoemaker, another part of Loaning Hill was occupied by the widowed Agnes Rogers, who struggled to make ends meet as a dressmaker. She had a long local pedigree for her grandfather was born in Kilmany in 1782, became the grocer and in his last years also took on the Post Office when it opened during the 1850s. In November 1915 her older son, Alexander, set out from here to join the Honourable Artillery Company. He was an under-gardener employed by the Anstruther-Grays, and is the only soldier from the hamlet of Kilmany who did not return. Having crossed to France in October 1916, he was killed in action six months later, having been promoted to Corporal in the field. He lies buried far from his family in the Pas de Calais.

INDEX

Aberdeen Assembly, 11
Adam family, 47, 51, 52
Agricultural improvement, 17, 19, 20, 22, 23, 54, 56, 96
Aitken family, 92
Amphitheatre, 1, 19
Anderson, George, 92
Angling, 22
Anstruther-Gray, Mrs, 73, 75
Anstruther-Gray, W., 69, 70, 71, 72, 73, 76
Anstruther-Gray, W. J. St C (see Kilmany, Lord)
Anstruther Thomson, J. (1776–1833) 19, 25, 27, 37, 43, 44, 47, 48, 49, 50, 51, 52, 56
Anstruther Thomson, Mrs, 47, 48, 49, 50, 51, 66, 68
Anstruther Thomson, J. (1818–1904) 49, 50, 52, 53, 56, 57, 58, 68, 69, 70
Baillie, Captain, 18
Balfour, Alexander, 90
Balfour, James, 90
Balfour, Sir James, 94, 95, 96
Balfour family, 8, 13, 38, 40
Ballinbreich, 9
Balmerino Abbey, 6, 7, 8
Balmerino, Lord, 18
Beaton murder, 8, 41, 43
Beeching, Dr, 83
Bethune, Colonel Harry, 43
Bethune, Mary Sharp, 43
Black Earnside battle, 7
Blacksmiths in the parish, 60. 72
Blair Adam Club, 51, 52
Blaeu's map, 22
Bluff, Norman, iii
Brewster, D., 59, 60
Broughty Ferry, 8

Brown, Mrs, 63, 83, 84
Bruce, Bishop, 8
Bruce, Robert, 76, 77
Buchan, John, 12, 19
Buses, 80
Calderwood family, 39
Carswell family, 89, 93
Chalmers, Thomas, 28, 29, 30, 31, 32, 33, 34, 35, 36, 37, 49, 66, 80, 96
Christie, Annie M'Donald, 97
Christie, David, 83, 98
Cill names, 4
Clark, Jim, 60, 78, 79, 96
Climate, 86
Coaching road, 45
Cook, H. D., 17, 18, 22, 23, 24, 27, 28, 36, 37, 42, 44, 90
Cook, John, 20, 21, 25, 27, 44, 46, 90
Covenanters, 13
Crawford, family, 39
Cruivie, 24 (lake), 35
Cuparmuir, 9
Cursus, 1
Dairy, 76, 85, 97
Darnley murder, 95
Defoe, Daniel, 13, 14, 15
de Varenne family, 6
Dewar, John, 91
Disruption 1843, 56
Drumnod, 37, 39, 95
Drumnod houses, 2
Duncan, Nathan, 71, 84
Dundee, earls of, 38
Easter Kilmany, 35, 37, 38, 43, 60, 70
Easter Kinnear, 3, 7, 11, 23, 37, 38
Edie family, 33, 34, 36
Edie, Robert, 33, 34, 35
Electricity, 79
Ermengarde, 6, 15
Estates, list of, 37

Fairies, 45
Fairlie, R. F. J, 73
Falkirk, 7
Falkland, 8
Female Industrial School, 60, 66
Feu duty, 19
Fife, earls of, 6, 7, 38
Fishing, 22
Flodden battle, 9
Fortified houses, 11
Fox Hunting, 47, 52, 53, 73
Gardener's Cottage, 85, 97
Ghoules' Den, 44, 45, 48, 50
Gillespie, David, (1774–1827) 25, 37, 40
Gillespie, David, (1814–1899) 41, 42, 43
Gillespie, David (d. 1911), 43
Gillespie, John, 39
Gillespie, Skipper Alexander, 39, 88
Gillespie Graham, J, 40
Glorious Revolution, 15
Grieve family, 71, 83, 84
Gypsy story, 66
Halkerston, Charles, 18
Halkerston family, 10
Halkerston, Helenus, 18, 88, 89
Hawkhill, 3
Haxton or Halkerston. David, 13, 14, 89
Haxton, John, 93
Hazelton Walls, 60, 92
Henderson, Alexander, 11, 66
Henderson, Ian, 80
Hendersons of Easter Kinnear, 6, 7, 96
Hillcairnie, 10, 37, 89
Horsburgh family, 91
Hugh of Kilmany, 7
Iron Age, 2
Jacobites, 18
James IV, 10
James VI, 10

Johnson, Samuel, 19, 24
Kilmany Bible Society, 66
Kilmany Church, 6, 8, 17, 27, 29, 30, 65, 80, 81
Kilmany Cottage, 48, 49, 52, 53, 68, 70, 98
Kilmany Curling Club, 66
Kilmany Flour Mill, 60, 61
Kilmany Free Church, 57, 58,
Kilmany Grange, 83, 98
Kilmany, House, 69, 72, 73, 85, 88, 98
Kilmany, Lady, 78
Kilmany, Lord, 77, 78
Kilmany place name, 4, 5, 6
Kilmany smithy (see also Wilson), 60, 65, 72, 80
Kilmany station, 74, 81, 87
Kilrymont (see St Andrews)
Kinnear family, 7
Kinnear, J. B., 38
Kirk family, 92
Knox, John, 8
Land holding, 37, 79
Leighton, Robert, 58, 59, 60
Leslie, Bishop, 1, 9
Letter box, 71
Leuchars, 6, 12
Lindsay, Alexander of Rathillet, 9, 93
Lindsays, earls of Crawford, 9
Lindsay, Sir David, 10
Lindores Abbey, 6, 7
Lindores hoard, 5
Loaning Hill, 20, 21, 54, 82, 84, 98, 99
Lochmalony, 18, 25, 37, 66
Lochmalony carved stone, 2
Logie, 58
Lucklaw Hill, 8
Lumsden, John, 60
Lumsden (Lumsdain) General Robert, 38, 39, 96
McGonagall, W., 63, 64, 85
Maitland, Barbara (Lady Gibson), 17
Malcolm IV, 6

Manor hall at Rathillet, 6
Manse, 36, 83
Margaret of Scotland, 5
Marriage lintel, 20, 21
Marshall, W, 71
Mary, Queen of Scots, 9, 10
McNab family, 78
Melville brass, 16
Meville, earl of, 15
Melville family, 10, 15
Melville, John of Cairnie, 15, 16
Melville, Mary, 15, 16, 17
Men's Club, 83
Mesolithic age, 1
Monmouth's Rebellion, 15
Mons Graupius battle, 2
Morton, 2
Motray, 5, 22, 23, 64
Motray Lodge, 85
Mountquhanie, 3, 8, 11, 22, 25, 37, 38, 39, 92, 94
Murdocarnie, 10, 15, 37
Murdocarnie, Lord, 10
Museum, 71, 82
Myrecairnie, 11, 37, 93
Myrecairnie, Lord, 11
Naughton, 6
New Road, 70, 92
Newbigging, 37
Newburgh and North Fife Railway, 73, 74, 75, 80, 81, 82, 86, 87
Nicolaisen, W. F. H., 4
Norman's Law, 2, 3, 5
Normans, 2, 3, 6
Occupations, 54, 55, 56, 60, 61, 71, 72, 79, 80
Parish Registers, 17
Paterson, Alexander, 33, 34, 35, 36, 96
Pearson, Captain, 27, 90, 91
Pearson family, 91
Picts, 3, 4, 5
Pilgrimage routes, 7

Pinkie battle and devastation, 8
Poems, 15, 16, 47, 53, 58, 63, 64, 93
Poor Relief, 32, 80
Population decrease, 56, 58, 83
Post Office, 60, 63, 71, 72, 80, 83, 84, 85, 97
Pococke, R., 1, 19
Prehistory, 1, 2
Pryde family, 54, 60. 71
Public baths, 73, 85
Railway, 74, 75, 80, 86, 87
Rathillet, 6, 9, 10, 11, 13, 14, 17, 18, 22, 31, 37, 60, 71, 72
Rathillet Church (Burgher, & later United Presbyterian), 56, 57, 80
Rathillet Cow Society, 66
Rathillet Mill, 7
Rathllet Old House, 14
Rathilletshire, 6
Robertson, James Thomson, 93
Roedeer, 8n., 50
Rogers, Alexander, 98
Rollo, Lord, 39
Romans, 2, 3
St Andrews, 3, 7, 9, 24, 70, 87
St Eithne, 4
St Fort, 75, 87
St Mannan, 4
Sandford, 3
Sawmill, 55, 56, 64, 72, 83
Schools, Hazelton Walls, 66
Kilmany, 60, 63, 64, 66, 85
Rathillet, 31, 60, 79, 80
Scott, Sir Walter, 51, 52
    Tree, 50
Scroggie, Jack, 81, 83
Secession Church at Rathillet, 56, 57
Shand, Jimmy, 76
Sharp, Archbishop murder, 13, 41, 43
Sharp, John, 11, 12, 89
Shepherd, The, 33
Sibbald, Sir Robert, 37, 38

Slave Trade, 32
Smibert, William, 18, 89, 96
Spy cartoon, 68
Squash court, 76, 85
Starr, 22, 38
Stevenson, Robert Louis, 13, 14, 17, 24
Stirton, 37, 39
Straggling huts, 20, 21, 54
Tay Ferry, 42
Tay Rail Bridge Disaster, 47, 48
Taylor, S., vii, 4
Thomson, John of Charleton, 19, 38
Thomsone, George, 12
Thomsone, James, 12, 13
Transport & Communications, 45, 46, 73, 80
Trees, 24, 25, 27
Union, Act of, 17
United Presbyterian Church (Secession), 57, 80
University of St Andrews, 7, 28, 37
Upwardly mobility, 54, 88, 93
Vikings, 5
Villagers, 61, 61, 62, 79, 80
Volunteers, 42, 47, 53,
War Memorial, 96
Watt family, 60, 72
Wedderburn family, 43
Weir family, 78
Wemyss family, 11
Wemysshall Hill, 9
Wester Kilmany, 37, 72, 76, 83
Wester Kinnear, 7, 37, 38
Whiteford family, 83
Wilson, Blacksmith in Kilmany, 60, 65, 72, 80, 84
Witches, 12, 13, 44, 45
Women's Guild, 83
Women's Rural Institute, 73, 83
Woodland, 24, 25, 83
Young, Eric, 76

www.ingramcontent.com/pod-product-compliance
Lightning Source LLC
Chambersburg PA
CBHW070619050426
42450CB00011B/3081